The Contemporary Med
in Practice

SPOTLIGHTS

Series Editor: Timothy Mathews, Emeritus Professor of French and Comparative Criticism, UCL

Spotlights is a short monograph series for authors wishing to make new or defining elements of their work accessible to a wide audience. The series provides a responsive forum for researchers to share key developments in their discipline and reach across disciplinary boundaries. The series also aims to support a diverse range of approaches to undertaking research and writing it.

The Contemporary Medieval in Practice

Clare A. Lees and Gillian R. Overing

First published in 2019 by
UCL Press
University College London
Gower Street
London WC1E 6BT

Available to download free: www.uclpress.co.uk

ISBN: 978-1-78735-467-8 (Hbk.)
ISBN: 978-1-78735-466-1 (Pbk.)
ISBN: 978-1-78735-465-4 (PDF)
ISBN: 978-1-78735-468-5 (epub)
ISBN: 978-1-78735-469-2 (mobi)
DOI: https://doi.org/10.14324/111.9781787354654

Contents

List of illustrations

Acknowledgements

We are grateful for the many forms of support, material and otherwise, that we have received throughout the slow collaborative making of this book, and we thank first our respective institutions. Clare thanks King's College London for supporting her work over many years and the School of Advanced Study, University of London, for the warm welcome and enthusiastic support she has received since she joined the Institute of English Studies in September 2018. A Major Research Fellowship from the Leverhulme Trust in 2016–18 was hugely beneficial to Clare's work: many thanks indeed. Gillian has been generously supported by Wake Forest University and wishes to thank the Office of the Dean of the College, her Chair, Jessica Richard, and Dean Franco, director of the Wake Forest Humanities Institute, for their support in the form of research and publication grants, leave time and, especially, commitment to collaborative work in the humanities.

This book would not have been possible without the many artists who have inspired it, participated in it, and been so generous with permissions to use their work. We thank Roni Horn. Her corpus of work on water has been the tide of our thinking. We carry with us her gifts of *Wonderwater* and *Ísland: To Place,* and regularly exchange them as we collaborate across the Atlantic. Caroline Bergvall has provided both inspiration and the invaluable opportunity to collaborate with her in various contexts. We thank the twelve poets on the bus to Lindisfarne for their inspiring and joyful perspectives: Gillian Allnut, Peter Armstrong, Linda Anderson, Peter Bennet, Colette Bryce, Christy Ducker, Alistair Elliot, Linda France, Cynthia Fuller, Bill Herbert, Pippa Little and Sean O'Brien. Thanks in particular to Linda Anderson and the Newcastle Centre for the Literary Arts, and to Tim Eastop, Ben Eastop and John Hartley of Difference Exchange. We thank Abraham Anghik Ruben for the urgent message of his breath-taking sculptures. We thank artist and poet Sharon Morris and Enitharmon Press for letting us include her work and for her generous collaborative input and presence. And we look forward to further explorations of medieval contemporary art with her, Neil Jeffries, Jayne Parker, Liz Rideal and Jo Volley.

Others have given us editorial support and encouragement in the writing and production of a book that takes some risks. We thank Tim Mathews of University College London for his early and ongoing enthusiasm for our project, and the editorial staff at UCL Press. An early version of Chapter 2 was given at the Leeds International Medieval Congress: we thank Catherine Karkov for that opportunity. Bob Mills provided welcome insight and perspective at just the right moment; conversations with Ed Fox and Alex Loftus continue to inspire. Mathelinda Nabugodi and Donna Beth Ellard have organized and participated in workshops that were an important part of the making of this book; we thank them and the workshop participants for helping us think about audience, and how to better connect with non-medievalists. We have been lucky to work with colleagues, students and former students of King's College London and Wake Forest University, with whom we have explored the idea of the contemporary medieval: thank you so much, Josh Davies, Mary Kate Hurley, Carl Kears, Sarah Salih and Ulrike Wiethaus, as well as James Paz, Fran Allfrey, Fran Brooks, Becky Hardie, Kath Maude, Hana Videen, Vicky Walker and Beth Whalley. And so, finally, we thank all our students – always the best sounding-board for how ideas can translate – and each other, for the long journey and continuing conversation.

1

Doing it differently: medieval and contemporary

This book puts into practice a shared idea about the 'contemporary medieval'. It brings concepts of what is 'medieval' and what is 'contemporary' together in a dynamic and fluid exchange, and it explores how past and present might be put into practice in an ongoing critical conversation. It reflects on disciplines and practices engaged by our work as medievalists long interested in modern critical theory, and offers some broader context for the contemporary medieval within the fields of medieval studies and creative-critical discourses in the arts and humanities. While we want this chapter to serve as an introduction to the book as a whole, we first offer an explanation and exploration of what we mean by 'contemporary medieval', why we think it is important and what it can contribute to our aim of working differently. The chapter concludes with a further reflection on its title, on what 'doing it differently' might mean.

First, and very briefly, we introduce ourselves and our way of working. We are both early medieval scholars with a long history of collaboration. Our subject is early medieval Norse and British culture (often termed Anglo-Saxon studies), c. 500–c. 1100, and we have a long-standing interest in and commitment to understanding the literary culture of this period in relation to genders and sexualities, places and locations, ecocriticism and environmental studies.[1] Chapter 2 outlines in more detail the winding path of our collaborative and individual research over some thirty years to reflect on the twists and turns of scholarly practice. Here we note simply that working together is central to our research, and so also to our rationale for the contemporary medieval. But where might we locate the beginning of this idea?

Twelve poets on a bus

It rained steadily that day. Clare was accompanying a group of poets to Lindisfarne in Northumberland as part of her work for *Colm Cille's Spiral* with the London Arts Agency, Difference Exchange. The project presented a re-imagination of the legacy of the sixth-century Irish monk Colm Cille, St Columba, through six contemporary art and literature commissions and dialogues that unfolded across Ireland and the UK as part of the City of Culture 2013, starting and ending in Derry-Londonderry, Northern Ireland. One particular 'knot' in the collaborative spiral linked Newcastle, Lindisfarne and nearby Bamburgh in an exploration of artistic innovation and the early medieval past. The commission of this 'knot', 'The Word', directed by Linda Anderson (Newcastle Centre for the Literary Arts), celebrated the natural beauty, deep history and artistic legacy of the early medieval kingdom of Northumbria by bringing it into engagement with the region's well-established reputation for modern and contemporary British poetry. This dual emphasis on place and cultural practice connected Newcastle with the tidal island of Lindisfarne, whose early medieval monastery was founded by St Aidan, and the Lindisfarne Gospels, dedicated to St Cuthbert of Lindisfarne, and with Bamburgh, the early Northumbrian royal city where Aidan died. Whence the poetry bus from Newcastle to Lindisfarne.[2]

Shadow Script: Twelve Poems for Lindisfarne and Bamburgh by Gillian Allnut, Peter Armstrong, Linda Anderson, Peter Bennet, Colette Bryce, Christy Ducker, Alistair Elliot, Linda France, Cynthia Fuller, Bill Herbert, Pippa Little and Sean O'Brien, edited by Colette Bryce, was published later in 2013.[3] The commission also produced a site-specific sound installation, *Antiphonal*, engineered from the commissioned poems and mixed with recordings of natural sounds and Old English words, by artist Tom Schofield (Culture Lab, University of Newcastle). *Antiphonal* was installed in the two locations of the crypt of St Aidan's Church, Bamburgh, and the then newly renovated Look-Out Tower on Lindisfarne. Two films by Kate Sweeney were then added to the sound installation, which previewed in Newcastle.[4] In 2013, *Shadow Script* and *Antiphonal* brought together Bamburgh and Lindisfarne for the Festival of the North East and the Lindisfarne Festival (when the Lindisfarne Gospels were displayed at Durham Cathedral). At the end of the year, 'The Word' participated in the culminating events of *Colm Cille's Spiral* in Derry-Londonderry, long associated with St Columba, Colm Cille, in the concluding days of its term as the UK City of Culture.

Clare had not been on a poetry bus before. She wasn't very familiar with tweeting either, let alone poets tweeting on a poetry bus. She was more comfortable with poets and writers who lived over a thousand years ago than those sitting next to her. And the weather was dreadful. It was hard to walk against the wind, let alone imagine the powerful motivations that had brought Aidan and later Cuthbert to Lindisfarne, ushering a new religion and culture into the region, or to hear the voices of those anonymous others – women, travellers and traders, warriors and farmers among them – who also contributed to this remarkable legacy of new practices and new words. And yet, for all that, it was fun – joyful, thought-inspiring and revitalizing.

As *Shadow Script* bears out, the modern poets also offered new visions, words and practices forged of an intense engagement with the local history of Northumberland and its poetry. Working together across disciplines and practices offered reflections on the creative vitality of the past and different ways to explore and share knowledge. One poem, 'Lindisfarne: The Roughs', by Gillian Allnutt, even got to grips with the weather, then and now.[5] Another equally remarkable poem, 'Asylum', by Colette Bryce, was to become part of Clare's chapter, 'In Three Poems: Medieval and Modern in Seamus Heaney, Maureen Duffy and Colette Bryce', for a collection of essays edited by Gillian together with Ulrike Wiethaus.[6] That collection, *American/Medieval: Nature and Mind in Cultural Transfer*, offered Gillian a chance to explore the wider dimensions of these tides of connection between the medieval and the contemporary in terms of deep exchanges at the level of history of ideas between the European medieval world and the USA. The focus on cultural and natural traces of this ongoing exchange is expanded in the forthcoming second volume, *American/Medieval Goes North: Earth and Water in Transit*, to explore ecocritical and environmentalist concerns, climate change and indigenous displacement.[7]

Colm Cille's Spiral has offered a number of other legacies. Several postgraduates and early-career scholars who worked on the project elaborated 'New Ways to Know the Medieval' in a short reflective article for the *Old English Newsletter*.[8] Some early medievalists, most notably Joshua Davies and Carl Kears, advanced or initiated related research projects of their own, exploring the medieval and the modern.[9] Clare contributed a brief prefatory paragraph to a second poetry pamphlet, *Waves and Bones*, in many ways a companion to *Shadow Script*, which was commissioned by the Newcastle Poetry Festival in 2018.[10] She wasn't able to make a second bus trip because of the weather (snow!). By then, however, learning more about contemporary poetry and its relationship with early medieval culture was central to her research. Between 2014 and 2018, while Clare was working and teaching with colleagues and students at King's College London, benefiting from a Major Research Fellowship from the Leverhulme Trust during 2016–18, and collaborating as ever, on and off, with Gillian, the shared idea of the contemporary medieval came into focus.[11] This idea depended from its beginning on working together and exploring new practices in which early medieval British culture and history might resonate differently with various contemporary communities.

The story of Clare and the poetry bus shows how, and why, we have been drawn to those who are themselves drawn to the early medieval world, to the new ways of seeing that they bring to our work and to our ways of working. Working together and collaboratively, we have continued to explore different formats and venues where we might explore the medieval and the contemporary. We have studied and worked with artists, artworks and creative practices in a variety of contexts. In 2014, for example, we collaborated on 'Deep Water Tales', a multimedia presentation for *Midsummer Water Day* (King's College London), in conjunction with the *Museum of Water* installation by Amy Sharrocks at Somerset House.[12] In 2015, we explored 'Sonic Illumination', a collaborative event at the Whitechapel Gallery, London, for *Adventures in the Illuminated Sphere*, directed by poet and multimedia artist Caroline Bergvall during her residency at the Gallery. Students and staff at King's College London participated in both events.[13] And, most recently, we have worked with poet and artist Sharon Morris on 'Putting the Audience into Practice', for the first Creative Critical Writing workshop (University College London, 2017). We also share a long-standing interest in the American artist Roni Horn, and a growing one in the Inuvialuit artist and sculptor Abraham Anghik Ruben. Reflecting on, responding to and exploring the implications of the very different practices of Bergvall, Horn, Morris and Ruben are central to our thinking about the contemporary medieval, as it travels across British, European, Inuit and American domains.

Early medievalists rarely work with experts in the contemporary arts, although there is a growing awareness of the importance of modern medieval literature, creative-critical writing and public arts practices for engaging with contemporary audiences.[14] The next section considers how and why we might bring together research-led fields such as ours with those fields committed to practice-based research or, more simply, practice research in the contemporary arts. Here, however, we use the story of the poetry bus to give a sense of what creative practices in the present might restore to our thinking about the past: a refreshed emphasis on the creativity of early medieval work, a renewed interest in the dynamic interactions between places and peoples, medieval and modern, a deepened commitment to exploring the different pathways between the present and the past, and an ongoing insistence on the value of shared work, collaborative thinking and participatory practice. The story of the poetry bus furnishes us with some of our key themes for this book: the weather (that rain) and the environment (those various relations between peoples and places), travel (the pathways between the present and the past) and the importance of reflection (creative and critical).

Reflections on disciplines and practices

Poetry, sculpture, photography, film and multimedia performance are some of the arts practices that we have brought to this book's interest in the contemporary medieval. In this regard 'contemporary' means produced now or in the very recent past. We work with living arts practitioners, and we explore live contemporary concerns and debates shared by many who work in the arts and humanities. We use our training as early medievalists to highlight the powerful but sometimes unacknowledged legacies of the early medieval past in these present, cultural, artistic and environmental issues. Our emphasis on practice, and on practice research, offers us a set of contemporary methodologies with which we might put the contemporary and the medieval into the same discursive space. This is also a space taken up by creative-critical work that similarly aims to explore the dynamic possibilities practice-led research offers theoretical reflection.[15]

The Contemporary Medieval in Practice, therefore, is informed by the three disciplines of medieval studies, in particular early medieval studies (as already noted), the contemporary arts and creative-critical work. It addresses the opportunity for the reformulation of trans-temporal, multidisciplinary and interdisciplinary thinking offered when these three disciplines are brought into relation. We conceive this relation as offering an emerging *environment* for interdisciplinary work within the creative humanities. We use this key term of 'environment' in different ways throughout the book to address the cultural, academic and ethical implications of working in the arts and humanities now: the physical environment, as used by cultural geography and the environmental humanities, and the discursive environment of areas and fields, the subjects and concepts of practices and ideas of academic disciplines more generally. Our second key term, *reflection*, also used in both literal and metaphorical senses, is threaded through the book, and informs in particular our choice of water as a subject central to Chapters 3 and 4.

Reflecting on collaboration and on multidisciplinarity more generally, however, we face questions about academic identities and about audience. Are we literary scholars, historians, medievalists, feminists, cultural theorists?, we are often asked. How can we speak through and across these categories or environments? And, to whom are we speaking? As our own field(s) and the humanities in general undergo sea changes, as the arts and humanities move in the direction of transdisciplinarity, indeed post-disciplinarity, these are shared issues. Challenged and inspired by recent research in the field of creative-critical writing and by the ethical direction of much contemporary arts theory, this book introduces new ways of developing transdisciplinary and transhistorical conversations. Chapter 2, 'Slow scholarship: the art of collaboration', aims to clear new spaces where we can talk to one another and to others in the humanities differently by reflecting on our past work and the deep history of the early medieval past which it engages. The chapter is informed by the structure of an interlace, a description of the early medieval artistic practice of linking and lacing that is found in visual, material and textual contexts. Famously, there is no beginning or end to the densely patterned interlaces of, for example, the early medieval illuminations of the Lindisfarne Gospels – a point we find helpful in describing the various ways our collaborative work has slowly circled around a set of ideas about gender, identity and the environment over the past thirty years or so. We have found contemporary, modern criticism about slow practices to be a useful analogue for the almost incomprehensible span of time involved in studying the early medieval past, in tracing its links and laces. The pressing urgency of reformulating time to understand the deep history of the environment and what contributions we can make to the study of the environmental humanities as contemporary medieval scholars is also central to this chapter, setting up a discussion we continue in Chapters 4 and 5.

Our reflecting on our own work in Chapter 2 is also an invitation to think about the various chronological periods in which the arts and the humanities are invested, those we study and those in which we participate as writers and teachers. We take this invitation in a different direction in Chapter 3, 'Audience: a prompt and three responses on falling'. To put the contemporary medieval into practice means thinking about how to access audiences for trans-chronological work. Our work over the last several years leaves us in no doubt that there is a significant contemporary audience for early medieval culture beyond our own academic environment of early medieval studies, which is rarely subject to analysis.

Accordingly, Chapter 3 explores how we might put the audience itself into practice. Using our experience of working with different audiences, the chapter offers three studies on ideas of audience, medieval and modern, prefaced by a prompt or call for response. We use these studies to inform the question of how might we be an audience for one another, and so fall into conversation.

Falling, however, may also entail failing. We are acutely aware of the incommensurability of our knowledge about early medieval culture on the one hand, and the contemporary on the other. Moving across times, disciplines and practices is a risky business, as Chapter 3 also explores, but with that risk come also possibilities of new ways of thinking and different directions. Chapter 4, 'Water: seven propositions for the contemporary medieval', takes up some of these possibilities. It is in this chapter that the different environments of the contemporary and the medieval are brought into direct relation. We reflect on the work of Horn, Ruben and Bergvall to open up further the kinds of critical and creative conversations we might have about the contemporary medieval, its places, environments and ambitions. The chapter focuses in particular on work by Roni Horn, who has no express interest in medieval culture, to challenge the apparent boundaries between the medieval, the medievalist and the modern. Medievalism, as a sub-discipline of medieval studies, draws on a set of wide-ranging disciplinary practices but tends to focus on work that is identified as 'medieval' in the post-medieval period. In Chapter 4, Horn's work, by contrast, occupies the fluid space between the creative and the critical, inspiring our reflections on both the medieval and the contemporary. Water, as Horn points out, is a 'master verb', and it also informs our analysis of the pathways between the early medieval past and the contemporary present more readily apparent in the arts practices of Ruben and the experimental poetry of Bergvall.

Chapter 5 continues to focus on environment, weather and water, but raises the stakes to ask some of the pressing questions about our contemporary relation to the environment that we also address in our final chapter. We explore the connections between early medieval and modern concepts of selfhood and look at how bodies and selves, historic and contemporary, are imbricated in environments and worlds. This chapter proposes a (be)coming together of self as matter and the material environment that we envision as a 'biodegradable self'. We explore this idea in some cultural contexts in early medieval Britain and Ireland, in the work of contemporary poets and artists who engage with the connection of identity and physical environment, and in the specific forms of Old English poetic language which allow the modern reader a new perspective on how the self is understood in deep symbiotic relation to the environment. Chapter 6 offers some final reflections on the contemporary medieval and our themes of self, environment, passage and translation, as we introduce the visions of some contemporary artists new to this project, Edward Burtynsky and M. NourbeSe Philip in particular. These are also artists with no direct connection to the medieval, but their work helps engage us in our conversation with the past; they speak to us both ethically and aesthetically across the divides of time, period and discipline, and urge us to put our valuing and understanding of the contemporary medieval into practice ourselves.

The trans-chronological, multidisciplinary focus of the contemporary medieval, therefore, requires moving beyond discipline-specific approaches to studying the medieval to address practice-based and creative-critical research: methodologies central to contemporary art and culture. Contemporary arts, both practice and methods, offer medievalists innovative ways to examine, explore and reframe the past. Medievalists offer practitioners of contemporary studies insights into cultural works of the past that have been made or re-worked in the present. Creative-critical writing invites the adaptation of scholarly style using forms such as the dialogue, the short essay and the poem. Similarly, each chapter of this book adapts a different form whose own history gives some indication of how current and medieval practices are co-implicated. We draw freely on interlace in Chapter 2, on call and response in Chapter 3 and on the propositional tract in Chapter 4, before settling back into more familiar academic prose to negotiate the discursive challenges of Chapter 5. We had wondered about other forms such as the dialogue, but realized that this book is informed instead by the idea of dialogue, or collaborative conversation, throughout. To return to the premise with which we began, the contemporary medieval is very much a shared idea.

Doing it differently

This book 'does' medieval studies differently by bringing it into relation with the field of contemporary arts and by making 'practice', in the sense used in the contemporary arts and creative-critical writing, central to it. Intersecting with a number of urgent critical discourses and cultural practices, such as the study of the environment and the ethics of understanding bodies, identities and histories, our study offers medievalists a distinctive voice in multidisciplinary, trans-chronological, collaborative conversations in the creative humanities. The scope of this book traverses the traditional and conservative field of Anglo-Saxon studies as it is still often understood by those within and without the field itself, and more radical and emergent contemporary forms of art-making and cultural practice. We aim to open up and define a creative-critical space where the medieval and the contemporary, fields often held apart, are brought into conversation with contemporary artists and their work in poetry and in the visual and material arts. We want to demonstrate that the study of cultural productions of the medieval in the contemporary opens up pathways of connection between the contemporary and the medieval different from those of, for example, medievalism, art history or literary and cultural history.[16] We want to develop new audiences among scholars, students and artists interested in working beyond disciplines and with creative-critical practices, and to challenge current modes of interdisciplinary thinking with conceptual categories that undo the boundaries underpinning disciplinary and interdisciplinary divisions. We also want to discover and encourage an audience within our own field, and to introduce medievalists to some expressions of contemporary art-making, including poetry, that they might not yet have encountered. We stress that we do this by way of exemplification, fully aware that there are many other ways to work across the contemporary and the medieval.

We recognize the importance of attending ethically to work in the past as well as the present: in the face of the troubling co-option of the medieval by the alt-Right in particular, however, we find that *The Contemporary Medieval* offers more creative, and optimistic, practices. We want to find a new language, or languages, in which to conduct our conversation with the past, in the hope that it inspires others to find their own languages, conversations and practices. Doing it *Together*, a work by Caroline Bergvall with which Chapter 4 concludes, prompts us to do it differently as well (see Figure 4.8).

A note on the past: Old English poetry

Some of our readers may have a passing familiarity with Old English poetry, others more detailed knowledge. The poems drawn on most often in this book are those best known to modern readers and scholars alike: *Beowulf, The Wanderer, The Seafarer* and the Old English riddles from the Exeter Book compilation of Old English poetry. We use the most accessible editions and translations throughout, and offer relevant, concise critical bibliography in the Notes. Like all early medievalists interested in the language of Old English, we work closely with the two major dictionaries of our field: the older *Anglo-Saxon Dictionary* edited by Joseph Bosworth and Thomas Northcote Toller, familiarly known as Bosworth and Toller and now available online, and the more recent, fully informed University of Toronto *Dictionary of Old English*, of which the letters A–I are, at the time of writing, available online.[17] Both resources have been invaluable.

While the study of Old English poetic metrics is almost a field in itself, we explain here briefly how we tackle formatting and translation. Old English poems are generally composed in half-line segments, and in each line the first half-line is aurally connected to the second by means of alliteration and syllabic patterns of stress, semi- or secondary stress and no stress. We follow editorial conventions by indicating the caesura between the two halves of a line with a space. A slash (/) in our translations into Modern English indicates the ending of the whole line, making the point that we are translating as literally, if inelegantly, as possible while still aiming for clarity. We use diacritics (e.g. macrons) where they are present in the specific editions we are quoting from, and elsewhere we have simplified, editing for sense and retaining the use of the variant letters æ Æ ('ash'), þ Þ ('thorn') and ð Ð ('eth').

Notes

1. In our individual and collaborative work, we have engaged with different branches and schools of contemporary critical theory. We have conceived our project here somewhat differently. While no single approach underlies this book, we continue to find ethical bases and inspiration for our thinking primarily in feminist and gender theory, as we outline in some detail in Chapter 2, as well as in ecocriticism and in place-based and cultural studies. In this book, however, we borrow more heavily from the ethical impulses underlying these theoretical categories than from any specific or overt meta-critical frame of reference.
2. See http://www.colmcillespiral.net/. Accessed 7 January 2019. And for the final project description see https://www.kcl.ac.uk/cultural/projects/archive/2013/colm-cilles-spiral. Accessed 7 January 2019.
3. *Shadow Script: Twelve Poems for Lindisfarne and Bamburgh*, ed. Colette Bryce (Newcastle University: Newcastle Centre for the Literary Arts, 2013).
4. See https://vimeo.com/katesweeney. Accessed 7 January 2019.
5. *Shadow Script*, 16–17.
6. Shadow Script, 4–5. See also Lees, 'In Three Poems: Medieval and Modern in Seamus Heaney, Maureen Duffy and Colette Bryce', in *American/Medieval: Nature and Mind in Cultural Transfer*, ed. Gillian R. Overing and Ulrike Wiethaus (Göttingen, Germany: V&R unipress, 2016): 177–201.
7. *American/Medieval Goes North: Earth and Water in Transit*, ed. Gillian R. Overing and Ulrike Wiethaus (Göttingen, Germany: V&R unipress, 2019).
8. 'New Ways to Know the Medieval: Creativity, Pedagogy and Public Engagement with *Colm Cille's Spiral*', by Francesca Allfrey, Francesca Brooks, Joshua Davies, Rebecca Hardie, Carl Kears, Clare Lees, Kathryn Maude, James Paz, Hana Videen and Victoria Walker, *Old English Newsletter* 46.3 (2015). http://www.oenewsletter.org/OEN/issue/46-3_allfrey.php. Accessed 20 January 2019.

9. Joshua Davies, *Visions and Ruins: Cultural Memory and the Untimely Middle Ages* (Manchester: Manchester University Press, 2018); Carl Kears, 'Eric Mottram and Old English: Revival and Re-use in the 1970s', *Review of English Studies* 69 (2018): 430–54.
10. *Waves and Bones* (Newcastle: Newcastle Centre for the Literary Arts, Newcastle University); part of 'Crossings: Newcastle Poetry Festival', 2018).
11. The MA module The Contemporary Medieval was first offered at King's College London by Lees and Sarah Salih in 2016 and covered both early and late medieval works and their modern, contemporary iterations. 'The Contemporary Arts and Early Medieval Culture in Britain and Ireland' was awarded a Major Research Fellowship by the Leverhulme Trust, 2016–18.
12. 'Deep Water Tales' was presented in the English Room as part of *Midsummer Water Day*; see https://www.kcl.ac.uk/search/search#/all?term=Midsummer%20Water%20Day. Accessed 29 May 2019. For the ongoing public arts project *The Museum of Water,* by Amy Sharrocks, see http://www.museumofwater.co.uk/. Accessed 7 January 2019.
13. Particularly noteworthy were the contributions of Joshua Davies to these events. For our work with Caroline Bergvall at the Whitechapel Gallery, see https://www.whitechapelgallery.org/events/adventures-in-the-illuminated-sphere/. Accessed 7 January 2019.
14. See, for example, Joshua Davies, *Visions and Ruins*, and Donna Beth Ellard, *Anglo-Saxon(ist) Pasts, postSaxon Futures* (Brooklyn, N.Y.: Punctum Books, 2019).
15. There is a growing literature about creative-critical writing; see, for example, *The Creative Critic: Writing as/about Practice*, ed. Katja Hilevaara and Emily Orley (London: Routledge, 2018).
16. For medievalism, See, for example, *The Cambridge Companion to Medievalism*, ed. Louise D'Arcens (Cambridge: Cambridge University Press, 2016), which does not include a chapter on the contemporary arts, however. Contrast Robert Mills's important study of *Derek Jarman's Medieval Modern* (Cambridge: D. S. Brewer, 2018).
17. *An Anglo-Saxon Dictionary*, J. Bosworth and T. Northcote Toller (Oxford: Clarendon Press, 1898) and *An Anglo-Saxon Dictionary: Supplement*, T. Northcote Toller (Oxford: Clarendon Press, 1921), available at http://bosworth.ff.cuni.cz. Accessed 30 January 2019. *Dictionary of Old English: A to I* online, ed. Angus Cameron, Ashley Crandell Amos, Antonette diPaolo Healey *et al.* (Dictionary of Old English Project, University of Toronto, 2018): https://tapor.library.utoronto.ca/doe/. Accessed 11 April 2019.

2
Slow scholarship: the art of collaboration

Comprising four interlinked strands, this chapter reflects on our own scholarly practice, collaborative and individual, over some thirty years. We employ the early medieval art of 'interlace' to characterize the trajectory of our work, and we structure this chapter as an interlace of its own, reworking the conventional scholarly essay to reflect the early medieval practices that inform our meditation.

The four strands are woven together in a kind of spiral or lace. We think of this structure as a linking together of our collaborative thoughts as well as a circling around them. Indeed, we are interested in exploring spirals, rings and laces, firmly part of the visual and verbal texture of early medieval culture, as figures of and for complex symbolic and cognitive processes. As many have pointed out, links, laces and knots in medieval visual culture are associated with the practices of rumination, 'ruminatio' in Latin: that is to say, contemplation and meditation in monastic textual culture. In much the same way, rings (Old English 'hringas') feature in the assembly of elite material objects (swords, necklaces, armrings and cups) described by Old English poetry and in the structure of the verbal art itself.[1] The making of elite early medieval art took time and was bound into spiritual as well as cognitive practices, as exemplified in the long dedication of Eadfrith, Bishop of Lindisfarne, to the writing and illumination of the early medieval Lindisfarne Gospels.[2] Contemplating now the many relationships between rings, laces and links – verbal and material – in early medieval culture is a pre-eminently slow practice. It too takes time, indeed demands it. Slow art, we argue, asks to be understood experientially through and over time; slow scholarship is a way to get at this understanding.

The modern, contemporary resonances of material culture in metaphors of thinking offer continuities with early medieval practices. Our thinking can still go round in circles, thoughts can still be knotty, things can still spiral, sometimes out of control, and some ideas may well be twisted. How medieval visual and verbal laces spiral, circle, ravel and unravel, entwine, knot, bind or blend seem to us, therefore, to be useful ways to think about practices of cognition and interpretation, about the processes of making (and remaking) meaning over time, now as well as then, together as well as apart. Another modern image for these cognitive, collaborative processes might be the double helix – and yes, the making of identity and environments, both of which contribute to that making, are important dimensions of our thinking over time and of our scholarship. Chapter 5 explores further the medieval interlacing of self and the environment; for now, we stay with reflections on our work.

Arguments for slow scholarship, for taking time, have surfaced in a number of disciplines in the arts and humanities in recent years. In the face of the urgencies of contemporary and future climate change, the environmental humanities make the case for slowing down and working together across disciplines. Working differently, ecocritics argue, enlarges the possibilities for engaged, historicized understanding and riskier thought even as time for the planet is running out.[3] Ecocriticism is one strand of contemporary slow scholarship that informs our own work on the early Middle Ages, which has increasingly connected contemporary and early medieval thinking about place and environment.[4] Another strand is offered by feminism, to which we have long been committed.[5] Contemporary feminist social and political thought has identified slowness, taking back time, as a way to resist forms of commodification and gendered identity in the academy and in the professional life of scholars and teachers.[6] Arguments for slow practices in the accelerated university have become focused on the publication of *The Slow Professor* by Maggie Berg and Barbara Seeber in 2016 and are not without controversy.[7] For some, advocacy of slow scholarship brings into focus sharp distinctions between the time enjoyed by full-time, employed or tenured academics and that available to those working precariously in part-time or temporary positions. Others counter that slow practices are ways for all academics to resist corporate emphases on research and teaching productivity, which often leaves little room for contemplative thought, long-term research and informed action about casualization on the one hand and acceleration on the other.[8]

Equally compelling as arguments for thinking about slow time from the environmental humanities and from feminism are contemporary arts practices. *Longplayer*, by Jem Finer, a digital musical composition that has been continuously unfolding since 31 December 1999 and aims to run for one thousand years, is permanently based at Trinity Buoy Wharf, London, with continuous online audio streaming. The hundred-year-long artwork *Future Library*, designed by Katie Paterson for Oslo, Norway, is another example of a public art project with duration, slowness, at the centre of its realization.[9] *Future Library* was initiated in 2014 with the planting of one thousand trees in Nordmarka, just outside Oslo; the eventual forest will supply the paper for the printing of an anthology of stories in a hundred years' time. Margaret Atwood deposited the first story in 2014, and others will follow until 2114. Until then the content of these annual literary depositions will remain unknown and unread, although their authors are identified. *Longplayer*'s compositional length of a thousand years presents an even more open-ended challenge to ideas of artistic completeness, finitude and technological mastery. Slow public artworks that unfold over time complement theoretical scholarly concerns with slow methodologies and practices in the arts and humanities: medievalists, we argue, have something to contribute to these interconnected conversations.

Future Library and Longplayer are examples of public arts practices that have longevity and duration built into them. They are also aimed at and focused on an unknowable future. Both introduce questions about technologies, temporal scale and audience into explorations of duration and slowness. Will *Longplayer* – a digital composition – be viable in a thousand years? How could we ever hear it, all of it? Will there be trees enough to sustain a *Future Library* in a hundred years? How will we know? Care for the arts and care for the environment are entwined with, laced into, these artworks and are projected into concerns about the future. Care and curation – the words are interlaced etymologically through the Latin 'curare' ('to cure'), and the Old English 'caru'/'cearu' ('sorrow, care') – are core practices for the contemporary arts. What, however, of our relation to the long past?

Similarly taking on the scale of human knowledge, our ability to read our world and concerns about our enduring relationship with our environments is Roni Horn's *Vatnasafn/Library of Water*, commissioned and produced by Artangel, an organization long committed to supporting the creation of artworks in unusual places.[10] This public artwork in a former library at Stykkishólmur in Iceland assembles three works in a single environment or place. *Water, Selected* is an installation of twenty-four glass columns that contain water collected from Iceland's many glaciers; the installation stands on *You Are the Weather (Iceland)*, a floor that features English and Icelandic words for the weather produced by Margrét H. Blöndal; another room features Horn's series of artists' books about Iceland, *Ísland: To Place*, and the collaborative archive on the Icelandic weather, *Weather Reports You*, which Horn describes as a 'collective self-portrait'.[11] Precisely because it works collectively in relation to the past and present of the environment, glaciers and the weather, language and shared narrative, *Vatnasafn/Library of Water* has offered us, long collaborators ourselves, different ways to frame our contemporary engagements with a chronologically distant past of some thousand to fifteen hundred years ago.

Glacial thinking, thinking about glaciers, laces deep time with our reflections on collaboration over time in this chapter.[12] Deep time was a core feature of early medieval science, associated with the calculation of time, its reckoning or *computus*, cosmology, the calendar, prediction, and meteorology or the weather. For examples, let us turn to the tenth-century writer, homilist and monk Ælfric, and before him the Latin scholar and monk Bede from the late seventh and early eighth centuries. Ælfric's 'lytel cwyde be gearlicum tidum' ('brief treatise on the times of the year'), *De temporibus anni*, which dates from the late tenth century, begins with the Christian Creation – the beginning of time in Genesis – and ends with accounts of rain, hail, snow and thunder. Bede's earlier treatises, on which Ælfric's partly rest, offer more detailed accounts of meteorology as well as of the motions of the tides. Celebrated for his calculation of the tides by relating ebb and flow to the lunar calendar, Bede described his *De temporum ratione* ('The Reckoning of Time') as 'a little book about the fleeting and wave-tossed course of time'.[13] In early medieval narratives about the environment, knowledge of time and the temporal order of things are complexly interrelated literally and metaphorically: Latin 'tempus', for example, refers to a season, a specific time, the temporal world and the weather.[14]

In exploring the collaborative methods of our scholarship in terms of a lace or a spiral, therefore, we have in mind material, artistic and interpretive practices that engage with knowledge of the world, medieval and modern. Our reflections have been brought into focus by recent explorations of slow scholarship, certainly, but are not coterminous with them; as we go on to explore in this chapter, we have been working together, slowly, for some time. By the same token, the term 'interlace', so well known to early medievalists, derives from post-Conquest contexts: it stands in for but does not replace a complex set of cultural associations between linking and locking, binding and weaving in the material and textual arts in the early Middle Ages.[15] There is no seamless way to link early medieval and modern usage here, even as we circle around material practices and cognitive processes, criss-crossing both in this chapter.

After all, understandings of the relationship between the slowness and circuit of time and the weather endure over the long term, as we have seen. The Old English noun 'gelac', with its associations with waves, motion and play (with its senses of playfulness as well as challenge), offers us a point of connection between the early medieval and the modern as we follow the movement of time, its play, its back and forth, its waves, to think through the slow process of reflecting on and engaging with early medieval culture.[16]

The time of our thinking

The nouns for 'time' in Old English and Latin, 'tíd' and 'tempus', offer ways to mark time, whether for an hour, a season, a moment or a duration. Similarly to uses in other medieval Germanic languages, Old English 'tíd' is also used to designate grammatical tenses, past or present. What, we ask in this section, has been, or is, the time of our thinking?

We have been working together for a long time. We started collaborating in the late 1980s and we have been working together on and off ever since. The time of our thinking in this sense spans some thirty years, we think. The *Medieval Feminist Newsletter*, now the *Medieval Feminist Forum*, itself in its early years in the late 1980s, was an important focus for our early work together. Following Gillian's lead, we collaborated with other scholars such as Helen Bennett and Karma Lochrie and participated in the debates around feminism and medieval studies in the early 1990s.[17] Our first co-authored article was published by the *Newsletter* in 1990 and we are grateful to see and to celebrate its growth and development from a modest paper newsletter to an international organization and a digital resource. When we started working together, we regularly found ourselves having to explain what it was that we did together. How, we were asked time and again, did we write? Who wrote what? Who said or did what? Who were the 'we' of whom we spoke? In 2001, a decade after our first collaborative article, we were still finding it necessary to address the question of what writing together means, and did so in the acknowledgements of our co-authored book, *Double Agents*.[18]

Single authorship has a powerful hold on the practice of scholarly writing. Experience teaches us to explain even now what we will do when we present a collaborative paper, reading separately sections that we wrote together. We reflect that our collaborative mode, whether written or spoken, calls forth in some a response that seems to want to unravel it into two distinctly, identifiably, separate strands. We, on the other hand, are far more interested in what happens when the thinking of two contributes to, evolves into, the making of one – one paper, one idea, one thought, whatever its origin. This, we thought in the early 1990s and still think now, is a form of feminist scholarly practice, informed as much by contemporary theoretical modes of the late twentieth and early twenty-first centuries as by our slowly increasing knowledge of the early medieval past. Women's writing in that period too is associated with collaboration.[19]

Now, we are long-standing feminist scholars – 'third-wavers', some might say – still interested in the same things, still finding ourselves returning to, circling round, similar questions, ideas and thoughts, and increasingly aware of the time of our thinking, of its temporal complexity and of its value to us as scholars. This process, we see now, might be identified as a form of slow scholarship, a form that values the taking of time to explore the complexity of the contemporary as well as the sophistication and multiplicity of the past, and that resists modes of scholarly practice that close off the past from its long engagement with the present. Here, too, feminism meets slow scholarship, for feminism, we are taught, comes in waves, like Vikings. There is in fact a persistent metaphorical association of new social movements with the movements of the sea, which we do not find particularly helpful, as each wave, or generation, is viewed as superseding – or drowning – the last. Perhaps we might use the language of wave theory to draw attention not to supersession but to intersection, reiteration and repetition, structures central to feminist thought and evident in slow practices as well.[20] We are reminded as well of Bede's description of temporal thought in terms of the sea, where the passing of time in *De temporum ratione* is 'wave-tossed' (Latin 'fluctiuago').[21] All this, of course, brings us to language, and to poetry in particular. Poetry knows its own temporality, one expression of which must be the fact that the time of its articulation is always expressed in the present, in the 'now' of its recitation and reading, however often it is read or spoken, and however old its language and expressive modes. In this sense, the time – and tide – of our thinking is now, as we think our way back into old poems and old thoughts. Old English 'tíd', we observed at the beginning of this section, means 'time', its marking, passing and tenses. Modern English 'tide', the motion of the sea, derives not from Old English but from Middle Low German, where Old English would use 'ebba' ('ebb') or 'flod' ('flood').[22] Which brings us neatly to the time and tide of our next section.

'Ofer ȳða ful': over the cup of the waves

Sometimes a phrase will haunt you for years, recurring in unexpected contexts, posing its questions differently, remaining an insistent and evocative puzzle. One such phrase begins our second section, and offers us an opportunity to ruminate on such 'haunting' as an aspect of slow scholarship, to explore our collaborative past and its imbrication with the present through the dimension of poetry. 'Ofer ȳða ful' means, literally, 'over the cup of the waves', or perhaps 'over the container of the waters', and is often just politely ignored by scholars and translated as 'the sea'. It's from *Beowulf*, line 1208.[23] The hero has just killed Grendel, there is a celebration in the hall, and Queen Wealhtheow, herself a cup-bearer par excellence (line 624), has brought the ceremonial drinking cup to Beowulf (line 1169). Among other rewards, she has given him a valuable neck-ring, and sandwiched in between her two speeches to Beowulf is the poet's recollection of the ill-fated story of Beowulf's lord and uncle, Hygelac, who will wear this great treasure when he, 'for wlenċo' (line 1206) ('out of pride'), goes raiding in Frisia and gets himself killed. Before Hygelac carries it off again, Beowulf must first carry the queen's precious bejewelled gift home, over the cup of the waves ('Hē ðā frætwe wæġ, / eorclanstānas ofer ȳða ful', lines 1208–9).

Many crossings over the waves and many exchanges, both literal and metaphorical, of cups and objects such as neck-rings are invoked by this passage of *Beowulf*. As we dive in to make meaning out of its linked chain of ideas, its rings and spirals of association, its collation of temporal dimensions, we acknowledge a level of affective experience of those metaphors of interlace that we invoked at the beginning of this chapter. Beowulf accepts the gift of the neck-ring from the queen, but must sail back to Geatland from Denmark and regift it, as a loyal thane should. He gives it to Hygd, and then it passes to her husband, Hygelac, before it embarks again – across the cup of the waves. The object of the cup, like so many other objects in the poem, is in motion, through and across temporal and geographical zones. There's Beowulf's present moment of glory (he has just killed the monster, Grendel) freighted with the image of the future and Hygelac's ignominious death, and of course with the weight of the past, as the poet has also made an elaborate comparison of this neck-ring to another very famous mytho-historical one, the necklace of the Brosings – whereby hangs another tale.[24] The queen, Wealhtheow, is in this associative maze, too. She is both chattel and chattel-giver, carrier of cups and rings and catalyst for their passage. This kind of multiple and imbricated meaning is the way the poem works, and those of us who have worked with it know well its frustrations and rewards. Interlaced in this mix of metaphors are the feminine, the heroic, the masculine, the idea of both motion and containment – there's that cup, not to mention that wave – and the connective and disjunctive presence of water. Which recalls another phrase – always the way in Old English – this time from another poem about travelling across water, *The Wanderer*: 'ofer waþuma gebind' (line 24), over which he must travel, however careworn.[25] The phrase means, literally, over the binding or fastening of the waves or waters; John C. Pope also suggests 'congregated waters', 'confinement of the waters', as well as 'waves' embrace'.[26] However we imagine this watery place, it is the Wanderer's milieu; these waters are the co-ordinates of his physical and intellectual voyage. The phrase conjures and constitutes venue, an idea of place that, although it is at once shifting and implacable, is the only venue to which he must regularly send his weary heart (lines 24, 57). Such unstill and complicated waters are not confined to oceans. They recall and echo another phrase, a compound in *Beowulf*, 'ȳð-ġeblond', 'wave-confusion, mixture, mingling, or commotion'. This one occurs three times in the poem (lines 1373, 1593, 1620) each time referring to Grendel's mother's watery home – so it's not just oceans, but inland meres too.

One thing, perhaps the only thing, one can say about water is that it is always plural, to quote contemporary artist Roni Horn (an idea to which we will return in Chapter 4).[27] However much we send cups and thoughts, ships or gifts, over it, weary hearts over it, heroes down into it, however much we try to bind, fasten, embrace or acknowledge its variousness, its motion and commotion, its back and forth, we cannot ignore its essential plurality that keeps meaning in play. To return to some of our core premises, then, we find that phrases such as these, and the practice of engaging with the pluralities that they demand, take us 'over the cup of the waves', over the 'wave-tossed course of time', and back again, into our collaborative spiral. They remind us not only of the kinesis of interlace, but of the energy, challenge and creativity of 'gelac', or play.

The patterns of our thought

As we reflect on our own modes of thinking in this chapter, we ask ourselves how the patterns and movements of our thinking over time might also help to address the question of how scholarship in the humanities evolves. What is slow, or, better, *slowed down*, in the progression, indeed the procession, of causes and effects and circumstances of our collaborative thinking? What is still opaque, what has become blindingly obvious, that we are still saying but not quite repeating? How might we understand the interlace or spiral (as opposed to circle) of our collaboration? This third strand reflects on and teases out some of the patterns, recursions and repetitions we found, and continue to find, in our thinking. Some forms of repetition are expansion and usher in new ways of configuring scholarly inquiry. One case in point is interlaced in our individual and collaborative thinking about gender.

Around the time we began working together, Gillian had published *Language, Sign and Gender in 'Beowulf'* (1990).[28] The 'gender' part of this book dealt primarily with women, a critical aporia in *Beowulf* criticism at the time. We hardly needed feminist theory, the book asserted, to tell us this was a poem about men – we had heard plenty about them already. Clare's rejoinder came in 1994 in the form of 'Men and *Beowulf*', in *Medieval Masculinities: Regarding Men in the Middle Ages*. Men, maleness and forms of masculinities, she pointed out, were far more complicated categories in the world of this poem, than Gillian, or indeed J. R. R. Tolkien, had allowed.[29] But there was a further aporia, both critical and intellectual. *Language, Sign and Gender* had also studiously avoided Grendel's Mother. Gillian winces to recall that she chose not to discuss Grendel's mother because she wasn't quite human, because 'her particular brand of otherness made it hard to distinguish between what is monstrous and what is human – a complication I considered less than useful to my argument.'[30] Gillian had been willing to take on the hybridity of the hero to some extent, but not the conundrum that she was later to call 'GM', Grendel's mother. Unlike Beowulf, and more like the stag on the bank who'd rather face its own hunters than take a dive into the 'ȳð-ġeblond', 'wave-confusion, mixture, mingling, commotion', she was not ready to enter the mere, with its underground hall or cave, home of Grendel and Grendel's mother.

Now let's fast-forward from the 1990s and the publication of Gillian's book on women and Clare's on men to our contemporary moment. In the intervening years, our work together and apart has wandered into various terrains but always with gender and place as our environment, providing ideological anchors as well as evolving critical and theoretical co-ordinates. We still situate the gendered self in relation to place, but we now ask broader questions about processes of embodiment and their environmental conditions – and about how these might all be interlaced with the connective tissue of water. One early genesis of our article 'Women and Water' developed Gillian's re-evaluation of Grendel's mother in '*Beowulf* on Gender' in 2010.[31] When she came to understand the centrality of GM's 'particular brand of otherness' and her presence as key to the evolving and shape-shifting formations of identity in the poem, GM's watery milieu, her hall under the mere, became downright inviting. But there was more work to be done. In Gillian's case, 'Women and Water' led to an examination of men and their relationship to weather, and the affective dysfunction of the troubled warrior, whose 'hreoh-mod' (stormy mind or inner turmoil) often has both literal and metaphorical continuity with that of the elements, with storms in the world. Here Gillian came full circle or, rather, continued the collaborative spiral. 'Men in Trouble: Warrior Angst in *Beowulf*' argues that male warrior anxiety has been explained away by invoking some critical arguments familiar in Old English scholarship.[32] In these critical accounts, the poem variously details a heroic culture in transition between pagan and Christian, or threatened by extinction, or it's an elegy for the heroic past, or a chronicle of loss. While these critical stances point to what underlies some of the poem's anxieties, ambiguities and cruces, if these dichotomies are resituated we might get closer to what troubles men. That culture in transition might be redrawn as a martial heroic ethos troubled by clerical, Christian culture, for example, creating an impossible quandary for poetic representations of the warrior male on several levels.

At this juncture, our collaborative thinking spirals back to an important piece of Clare's argument in 'Men and *Beowulf*' from 1994, namely that the concerns of the warrior elite – to replicate itself, to create and control sameness, to ensure succession and maintain power – are also modes that are vital to our understanding of masculinity in the poem.[33] So, too, is the crippling anxiety that these modes must produce, as Gillian argues in 'Men in Trouble'. As these strands of our collaborative and individual thinking intersect, we gradually widen the context for understanding the social and psychic production of masculinity; we bring weather and culture together. These troubled men, and Beowulf is only one of them, *are* the weather, to paraphrase Roni Horn's 'You are the Weather (Iceland)' in the *Library of Water*.[34] The 'hreoh-mod', the inner storm, reflects, embodies, the weather of the poem, if we insist that what we mean by 'environment' is both visceral and conceptual, and that it can encompass the cultural, political and physical worlds of this and other Old English poems.

Clare has also continued the spiral of our thinking. 'A Word to the Wise: Men, Gender, and Medieval Masculinities' considers how structures of masculinity, co-constructed in relation to rank or status and family or kin, intersect also with the generic imperatives of instructional, or conduct, literature. The essay widens the context and the circle of our investigations into gender and masculinity once again to include early medieval wisdom literature such as the Old English poem *Precepts*. Analysing apparently 'untroubled' male relationships, and how the men of the secular elite, noble sons, are to be trained in the ways of the world and of virtuous living by their fathers, she explores aspects of performative masculinity. The 'mild' and 'pleasant' tone of *Precepts*, she concludes, lays bare the working of its own reproduction of a masculine, paternal and patriarchal Christian wisdom reproduced across the generations in the voice and in the name of the father.[35] Whether men are to be mild and pleasant as in *Precepts*, or find themselves troubled and stormy-minded as in *Beowulf*, the language of emotion turns on the language of the weather. We will develop this point further in Chapters 4 and 5, but reflect here on the intertwined patterns of our thinking, whether our work is produced collaboratively or separately.

Thinking over time

Whether we are contemplating the passage of the cup in *Beowulf* or catching a wave in feminism, as we trace the call and response of these critical movements in gender theory and in our own work, the spirals and intersections of interlace have been essential to our thinking over time, and about time. Perhaps the metaphors we study and think through shape our thinking, as we aspire to understand early medieval modes of cognition. *Beowulf* makes the case in point for us; it is a long and complex poem. It takes time to read, translate and figure out – and this is part of its interpretive pleasure as well as its aesthetic. If we were to imagine a performance context for this poem, it would have to be a lengthy, immersive one, whether performed all at once, over a period of days, or called upon for particular social, communal occasions, in part or in whole. Anglo-Saxonists have long explored the epic power of *Beowulf* in relation to the feats of memory and performance of twentieth-century oral poets. We have yet to think through, however, the critical race implications of this appropriation of, for example, modern oral poetry.[36]

As the poem moves, so have we. We understand and value the importance of repetition, recycling and return in our modes of thinking together over time. But our conversations and exchanges are never exact repetitions, never static. As we have just noted, Gillian's work on women in *Beowulf* prompted Clare's on men, as well as a whole co-authored book on women and the doubleness of clerical culture in Anglo-Saxon England, and we have returned to these topics again, separately and collaboratively. Our thinking for this book now takes place in the wake of the recent resurgence of feminist theory and practice within and without the academy, as well as a complementary return to masculinity studies.[37] Although we have seen our work associated with several different theoretical 'waves', we are well aware, as all Anglo-Saxonists are, that time and tide are the same thing, and wait for no-one. We do not think that counting waves is the only way forward. Rather, the movement of our thoughts, back and forth, is perhaps best – and perhaps only – understood *over time*, and *by taking time*.

Slowness is no bad thing, however much it might be associated with a lack of progress, a failure to keep up or move on. Some modern commentators have been saying much the same thing, as we pointed out at the beginning of this chapter. Slow, attentive reading, patient engagement with verbal artefacts, perhaps especially old, complex and sophisticated ones in their original languages, are increasingly important skills: they complement the practices of big data, distant reading and digital surfing. Attending to the metaphors at work in practices of slow, immersive learning brings us back to those Beowulfian cups and forward to our most recent publications, where we have been following the deep tides and eddies of transfer between the medieval and the contemporary.[38] Our thinking aspires to be even slower and broader, seeking immersion in a deep time that enfolds temporal and spatial dimensions, where gender and identity are in flux and creation, and thoroughly imbricated with environment.[39] A privileged artefact such as a cup can pass through feminine as well as masculine modes as well as the space over which it passes (Wealhtheow passes the cup in the hall; Beowulf must carry it over the sea). The binding of waves and the commotion of water call attention to the complex, and sometimes troubling, interrelation of mind, mood, place and gender. And the apparent stasis of ice evokes the deepest of time.

In 2001 in *Double Agents*, our collaborative book on the shadowy relationship, or perhaps the riddle of the relationship, of women to early medieval clerical culture, we were already thinking about the interrelation of identity, metaphor, absence – and ice. There we were particularly interested in the 'mater et filia' ('mother and daughter') riddle that takes water and its ice as subjects.[40] We will work again with Old English riddles in Chapter 4, especially those imaging the passage of water and the movement of ice, creating our own, albeit shorter, connection to the glacial thinking with which we began this chapter. Projects like Katie

Paterson's *Future Library* and Jem Finer's *Longplayer* conjure unimaginable duration and an unknowable future, but we have been asking the question of our relation to the long past, inspired by the curation of glacial water in Roni Horn's *Vatnasafn/Library of Water*. In 2007, the same year in which Horn assembled the *Library of Water*, Katie Paterson took sound recordings from three glaciers in Iceland, pressed three records which were cast and frozen using the meltwater of these glaciers, and played them simultaneously until they melted.[41] Both artworks address the increasing loss of glaciers in Iceland and relate this loss to ideas about how to record, store and care for our environment. In December 2018, Icelandic artist Olafur Eliasson worked with geologist Minik Rosing to bring *Ice Watch* to the Tate Modern, London. The installation, part of a series begun in 2014, was comprised of twenty-four blocks of ice cut from the same glacier, the Nuup Kangerlua Fjord in Greenland, arranged to resemble an ancient stone circle.[42] Here too the artwork calls public attention to the urgency of climate change, again interlacing care for the environment and the curation of culture. These contemporary routes to glacial thinking suggest that the Old English riddles, and Old English poetry overall, can open up to us not only a practice of slowing down but also one of rearranging time, of using the contemporary to inspire further work on the past.

Finally, then, our reflections in this chapter are less an argument for slow scholarship, however much it is informed by this practice, than for perceiving time differently, for creating and inhabiting a scholarly intellectual mode that allows for the idea of the passage of time, of time as passage, as crossing, as wave and tide, and for the collaborative mode as both twist and turn, link and lace. The time of our thinking. Over the cup of the waves. The patterns of our thought. Thinking over time. The metaphors we study do indeed create our modes of thinking – and that's no bad thing. Beowulfian and early medieval models of thinking remain remarkably appropriate in this digital present, offering us a call, if not to slow down, then to recalibrate the operation of time in our scholarly habits of thought, and to recognize the absolute necessity of so doing.

Notes

1. The most celebrated example of the practice of 'ruminatio' is in Bede's description of Cædmon's composition of Old English songs or poetry. Cædmon ruminated on the accounts of Scripture that were reported to him as if he were chewing the cud ('quasi mundum animal ruminando'); see Bede, *Ecclesiastical History of the English People*, Book IV, chapter 24, ed. B. Colgrave and R. A. B. Mynors (Oxford: Clarendon Press, 1969; rev. edn Oxford University Press, 1991), and for a useful analysis Gernot Wieland, 'Cædmon, the Clean Animal', *American*

Benedictine Review 35.2 (1984): 194–203. For the importance of ring composition or 'envelope' patterns in Old English poetry, see, for example, John D. Niles, 'Ring Composition and the Structure of *Beowulf*', *PMLA* 94.5 (1979): 924–35. The classic article on interlace and Old English remains the much-anthologized article 'The Interlace Structure of *Beowulf*' by John Leyerle, first published in the *University of Toronto Quarterly* 37.1 (1967): 1–17; for a recent, more comprehensive study see Megan Cavell, *Weaving Words and Binding Bodies: The Poetics of Human Experience in Old English Literature* (Toronto: University of Toronto Press, 2016).

2. See Michelle Brown, *The Lindisfarne Gospels: Society, Spirituality and the Scribe* (London: British Library, 2003).

3. See, in particular, Hannes Bergthaller *et al.*, 'Mapping Common Ground: Ecocriticism, Environmental History, and the Environmental Humanities', *Environmental Humanities* 5.1 (2014): 261–76.

4. See, for example, the essays collected in *A Place to Believe In: Locating Medieval Landscapes*, ed. Clare A. Lees and Gillian R. Overing (University Park: Pennsylvania State University Press, 2006). See also Gillian R. Overing and Marijane Osborn, *Landscape of Desire: Partial Stories of the Medieval Scandinavian World* (Minneapolis: University of Minnesota Press, 1994).

5. See, for example, Clare A. Lees and Gillian R. Overing, *Double Agents: Women and Clerical Culture in Anglo-Saxon England* (Philadelphia: University of Pennsylvania Press, 2001; rev. edn Cardiff: University of Wales Press, 2009).

6. See the influential article by Rosalind Gill, 'Breaking the Silence: The Hidden Injuries of the Neoliberal University', in *Secrecy and Silence in the Research Process: Feminist Reflections*, ed. Rosalind Gill and Róisín Ryan-Flood (Abingdon, Oxfordshire: Routledge, 2010), 228–44. See also the collaborative article by Alison Mountz *et al.*, 'For Slow Scholarship: A Feminist Politics of Resistance through Collective Action in the Neoliberal University', *ACME: An International Journal for Critical Geographies* 14.4 (2015): 1235–59.

7. Maggie Berg and Barbara K. Seeber, *The Slow Professor: Challenging the Culture of Speed in the Academy* (Toronto: University of Toronto Press, 2016).

8. See Mark Carrigan and Filip Vostal, 'Not So Fast! A Critique of the "Slow Professor"', *University Affairs/Affaires universitaires*, 22 April 2016. http://www.universityaffairs.ca/opinion/in-my-opinion/not-so-fast-a-critique-of-the-slow-professor/. Accessed 26 January 2019. See also the response by Alison Mountz *et al.*, 'All for Slow Scholarship and Slow Scholarship for All', *University Affairs/Affaires universitaires*, 9 May 2016. http://www.universityaffairs.ca/opinion/in-my-opinion/slow-scholarship-slow-scholarship/. Accessed 26 January 2019. See also Berg and Seeber, *The Slow Professor*. We note too *Slow Scholarship: Medieval Research & the Neoliberal University,* ed. Catherine E. Karkov, Essays and Studies 20 (Cambridge: D. S. Brewer for the English Association, 2019), which appeared too late for our full consideration here.

9. For Jem Finer's *Longplayer*, commissioned by Artangel and now supported by the Longplayer Trust, see http://longplayer.org/about/. Accessed 26 January 2019. For *Future Library* by Katie Paterson, see http://www.futurelibrary.no/. Accessed 26 January 2019.

10. See https://www.artangel.org.uk/about_us/. Accessed on 26 January 2019. Artangel also commissioned *Longplayer*.

11. For Roni Horn, *Vatnasafn/Library of Water*, see https://www.artangel.org.uk/project/library-of-water/. Accessed 26 January 2019. Blöndal is also the figure photographed by Horn twice for the sequences *You Are the Weather* (1994–5 and 2010–11), discussed by Clare A. Lees and Gillian R. Overing in 'Women and Water: Icelandic Tales and Anglo-Saxon Moorings', *GeoHumanities* 4.1 (2018): 97–111.

12. Another, different example of a medievalist engaging with the environment, past and present, is offered by Jeffrey Jerome Cohen, *Stone: An Ecology of the Inhuman* (Minneapolis: University of Minnesota Press, 2015).

13. *Ælfric's De Temporibus Anni*, ed. and trans. Martin Blake (Cambridge: D. S. Brewer, 2009), 76. For Bede's *De natura rerum* and *De temporibus*, see *Bede: 'On the Nature of Things' and 'On Time'*, trans. Calvin B. Kendall and Faith Wallis (Liverpool: Liverpool University Press, 2010), and for his *De temporum ratione* see *Bede: 'The Reckoning of Time'*, trans. Faith Wallis (Liverpool: Liverpool University Press, 1999), xvi.

14. For a related study, see Carl Phelpstead, 'Beyond Ecocriticism: A Cosmocritical Reading of Ælfwine's Prayerbook', *Review of English Studies* 69.281 (2018): 613–31.

15. See Cavell, *Weaving Words and Binding Bodies*.

16. For a related discussion of interlace and motion, modern and medieval, see Lees, 'Basil Bunting, *Briggflatts*, Lindisfarne, and Anglo-Saxon Interlace', in *Anglo-Saxon Culture and the*

Modern Imagination, ed. David Clark and Nicholas Perkins (Cambridge: D. S. Brewer, 2010), 111–28.

17. Gillian was practising and researching collaborative writing strategies in 'Writing across the Curriculum: A Model for a Workshop and a Call for Change', co-written with Cynthia Caywood, in *Teaching Writing: Pedagogy, Gender, and Equity*, ed. Cynthia Caywood and Gillian R. Overing (Albany: State University of New York Press, 1987), 185–200. The first issue of the *Medieval Feminist Newsletter* was published in 1986. See Helen T. Bennett, Clare A. Lees and Gillian R. Overing, 'Anglo-Saxon Studies: Gender and Power: Feminism in Old English Studies', *Medieval Feminist Newsletter* 10 (1990): 15–24; see also Karma Lochrie, Clare A. Lees and Gillian R. Overing, 'Feminism within and without the Academy', *Medieval Feminist Newsletter* 22 (1996): 27–31.

18. Lees and Overing, *Double Agents*, ix. We celebrated our ongoing collaboration when it was republished by the University of Wales Press in 2009, at p. xi in the preface, which also notes that we continue to circle round the same commitment to exploring women's relation to culture in the early Middle Ages.

19. See Clare A. Lees and Gillian R. Overing, 'Women and the Origins of English Literature', in *The History of British Women's Writing, 700–1500*, ed. Liz Herbert McAvoy and Diane Watt, History of British Women's Writing 1 (New York: Palgrave Macmillan, 2012), 31–40.

20. For wave theory and the history of feminism, See, for example, Linda Nicholson, ed., *The Second Wave: A Reader in Feminist Theory* (London: Routledge, 1997), and R. Claire Snyder, 'What is Third-Wave Feminism? A New Directions Essay', *Signs* 34.1 (2008): 175–96. For a useful introduction to intersectionality see Nina Lykke, *Feminist Studies: A Guide to Intersectional Theory, Methodology and Writing* (London: Routledge, 2010).

21. *Bede:'The Reckoning of Time'*, trans. Wallis, xvi.

22. 'tide, n.'. *OED Online*. June 2018. Oxford University Press. http://www.oed.com/view/Entry/201809?rskey=w8ttos&result=1&isAdvanced=false. Accessed 25 June 2018.

23. All references to *Beowulf* are to R. D. Fulk, Robert E. Bjork and John D. Niles, eds, *Klaeber's 'Beowulf' and the Fight at Finnsburg*, 4th edn (Toronto: University of Toronto Press, 2008). Translations are our own, unless otherwise indicated.

24. See *Klaeber's 'Beowulf' and the Fight at Finnsburg*, ed. Fulk *et al.*, for discussion of the history of the neck-ring, lines 193–4.

25. References to *The Wanderer* are from *Old English Shorter Poems. Volume II: Wisdom and Lyric*, ed. and trans. Robert E. Bjork, Dumbarton Oaks Medieval Library 32 (Cambridge, Mass., and London: Harvard University Press, 2014), 2.

26. *Eight Old English Poems*, ed., with commentary and glossary, John C. Pope and R. D. Fulk, 3rd edn (New York: W.W. Norton, 2000), 170.

27. *Saying Water (The River Thames, for Example)* by Roni Horn. CD (New York: Dia Center for the Arts, 2001).

28. Gillian R. Overing, *Language, Sign, and Gender in 'Beowulf'* (Carbondale: Southern Illinois University Press, 1990).

29. Clare A. Lees, 'Men and *Beowulf*', in *Medieval Masculinities: Regarding Men in the Middle Ages*, ed. Clare A. Lees (Minneapolis: University of Minnesota Press, 1994), 129–48, took Tolkien's celebrated essay, '*Beowulf*: The Monsters and the Critics', as its point of departure. Famously, Tolkien does not take on Grendel's mother in this essay.

30. Overing, *Language, Sign, and Gender in 'Beowulf'*, 81.

31. '*Beowulf* on Gender', *New Medieval Literatures* 12 (2010): 1–22; Lees and Overing, 'Women and Water: Icelandic Tales and Anglo-Saxon Moorings'.

32. 'Men in Trouble: Warrior Angst in *Beowulf*', in *Rivalrous Masculinities: New Directions in Medieval Gender Studies*, ed. Ann Marie Rasmussen (Notre Dame, Ind.: University of Notre Dame Press, 2019), 27–41.

33. Lees, 'Men and *Beowulf*', 149–6.

34. *You Are the Weather* is also the title of an earlier work of 100 photographic portraits of the same woman, Margrét H. Blöndal, emerging from various hot springs and pools in Iceland in 1994–5; for images, see Horn's *You Are the Weather* (Zurich: Scalo, 1997); see also note 11 above.

35. See Clare A. Lees, 'A Word to the Wise: Men, Gender, and Medieval Masculinities', in *Rivalrous Masculinities*, ed. Rasmussen, 1–26, at 19. For *Precepts*, see *Old English Shorter Poems*, vol. II, ed. Bjork, 20–7, with the references to mild words and a pleasant thought at lines 44, 60.

36. See, for example, John Miles Foley, *Traditional Oral Epic: The Odyssey, Beowulf and the Serbo-Croatian Return Song* (Berkeley: University of California Press, 1991).
37. As exemplified by the #MeToo movement, which has also reverberated within Anglo-Saxon studies. For the academic resurgence of interest in masculinities, See, for example, Rasmussen, ed., *Rivalrous Masculinities*.
38. See Clare A. Lees, 'In Three Poems: Medieval and Modern in Seamus Heaney, Maureen Duffy and Collette Bryce', and Gillian R. Overing and Ulrike Wiethaus, 'Introduction: The Making of American/Medieval', both in *American/Medieval: Nature and Mind in Cultural Transfer*, ed. Overing and Wiethaus (Göttingen, Germany: V&R unipress, 2016), 117–201 and 9–23 respectively.
39. Gillian discusses this entanglement of bodies, space and time in '*Beowulf*: A Poem in Our Time', in *The Cambridge History of Early Medieval English Literature*, ed. Clare A. Lees (Cambridge: Cambridge University Press, 2013), 309–31. Clare's editorial vision for this volume of the *Cambridge History* likewise reflects a broad trans-chronological and transhistorical approach.
40. See our discussion of Exeter Book Riddle 33, with its solution of 'iceberg', in *Double Agents*, 103–4.
41. Katie Paterson, *Langjökull, Snæfellsjökull, Solheimajökull*, 2007. http://katiepaterson.org/portfolio/langjokull-snaefellsjokull-solheimajokull/. Accessed 26 January 2019.
42. For an account of *Ice Watch* in London, see https://www.tate.org.uk/whats-on/tate-modern/exhibition/olafur-eliasson-and-minik-rosing-ice-watch. Accessed 29 December 2018.

3
Audience: a prompt and three responses on falling

A prompt

In Chapter 2, we took our time. We reflected on our scholarship over the past thirty or so years and interlaced ideas derived from early medieval culture into the strands of our reflection. We also took inspiration from modern public arts practices that are similarly involved in the slow arts. In dialogue with early medieval times, then, we argued that our times now call for a recalibrated understanding of the temporal in the light of slow scholarship, creative practice and self-understanding.

Chapter 3 takes this call for recalibration into another area of enquiry central to scholarly and creative practice: audience. We are interested in thinking further about those who might comprise our audience, those who – like us – read, listen, engage with and respond to practices that work across the various disciplines of the arts and humanities. What might we, whoever 'we' are, learn from each other, our audience? Who is, or might be, the audience for the contemporary medieval? And how might we figure audience into our critical work?

While Chapter 2 adapted the structure of interlace, Chapter 3 uses that of prompt and response. We think of this structure as a script for modelling how audience might be built into creative-critical practice, as we discussed in Chapter 1. A prompt calls forth a response, triggering associations not just with dramatic performance but also with other long histories of calling and responding – antiphons, chants, songs – practised by specific communities, both worldly and spiritual. Awareness of audience takes many different forms, and in prompting you to read our three responses, we hope we are able to gesture towards some of this variety.[1]

Prompted ourselves to think about audience, we first consider, in a very practical way, the language of audience in English; we use our second response to initiate a critical conversation about audience using material drawn from early medieval, late medieval and modern sources; and our third reflects on the practice of conversation itself, which will lead to the propositions about the contemporary medieval we offer in Chapter 4.

Questions of audience matter, whether to early medievalists, contemporary cultural critics or arts practitioners, who – like us – wish to share their work with others who also have questions about the past and its engagement in the present. Using our disciplinary knowledge while reaching out to different audiences requires a bit of stretch – or, if you prefer, a leap – beyond our disciplinary training in a specific set of scholarly practices into areas of knowledge informed by priorities, skills and training with which, by definition, we are less familiar. It also requires consideration of access. Journal editors and publishers are not always comfortable with scholarship that speculates and takes risks in its quest to find new readers and audiences, though this is slowly changing. In our own experience, we have been fortunate to have found direction and encouragement at UCL Press. Indeed, creative-critical practices, creative non-fiction and speculative criticism are research-led genres that resist normative assumptions about academic fields, the expectations of readers and the predicted audiences for books and articles. Working with different audiences is often understood to mean public audiences, outside the academy. This is a practice long embedded in arts practices as well as critiqued by them, particularly by those interested in the public arts.[2] Questions of audience have also been explored in policy debates about the 'value' of the creative and cultural industries.[3] In medieval studies, public audience is usually thought of in terms of outreach, impact or engagement in the UK and the public humanities in the USA. There's a growing interest in tracking the public uses of the medieval evidenced in the mass media, especially in its popular, political and frequently erroneous appropriations.[4] Thinking through these perspectives on audience – creative, policy-led, the public medieval – and working with a variety of audiences outside our own fields offers access to new modes of understanding and reflection.[5] For all these reasons, this chapter addresses the contemporary medieval by putting the audience into critical practice. However, the stretch or leap between disciplines and practices required to reach different audiences might take us in the direction of interdisciplinarity or of dilettantism. Either way, we risk falling. And so our three interconnected studies or responses explore the risks of falling – and failing – between disciplines and practices.

We are aware of the paradox this chapter presents. We aim to set in motion a creative-critical reflection on audience – using examples drawn from poetry, performance and images selected from different times, media and practices – in the full knowledge that you, our reader, indeed our audience, are our silent partners in this enterprise. How then might we engage you? One way is our use of the direct form of address, as you will have already noticed – a style still unusual in academic writing. By making the rhetoric of the written address explicit, we invite you to think with us, to respond to our reflection and to share our project. Silent audiences are nothing new, although it is worth remembering that expectations about silence, whether in reading or responding to performance, vary historically and culturally. While silent reading was a phenomenon worthy of comment in the late antique and early medieval centuries in the West, silence as a meditative, reflective practice has a broader transcultural and a deeper historical reach.[6] Meditation and silence are central to reflection and learning in many cultures, and silence is an active component of any discussion of audience as well. We are aware too, however, that silence can be a form of resistance as well as assent, a strategy for co-optation rather than a practice of meditative learning and immersive reflection.

We have put into practice our ideas about audience before. We first worked with ideas about audience for a creative-critical writing workshop organized by Mathelinda Nabugodi (University of Newcastle) and Timothy Mathews (University College London) at University College London in 2017. In London, we were joined by artist and poet Sharon Morris (Slade School of Fine Art, University College London), whose poetry – and insights – feature in the second of our responses here. Our audience for this workshop comprised over forty researchers and teachers, early-career academics and postgraduates drawn from different disciplines in the arts and humanities. The event subsequently proved to be the first in a series of creative-critical writing workshops organized by Nabugodi and Mathews, and as the only medievalists at that first meeting we wondered whether medievalists might be said to be more hesitant than other disciplines to participate in a multidisciplinary creative humanities. We reworked the same material for a workshop in 2018 at Denver University, although this time without the presence of Sharon Morris and her critical and creative input. Here we were joined by an audience of postgraduate students, medievalists, creative writers and other academics from the departments of modern languages and English at Denver University. Donna Beth Ellard, an early medievalist and creative writer herself, was our host. This was a smaller audience than that in London and one whose knowledge of medieval culture was in some cases more established. As in London, however, this group was alert to the challenges of thinking about audience from the perspective of creative-critical, transdisciplinary practices. Each of these workshops engaged a particular audience in questions about 'audience' in a collaborative space. In each we used a variety of techniques, including short presentations, exercises in reading, silent reflection, dialogue and group work to elicit a creative-critical conversation that took place in real time (that is, to say, the academic time of a workshop, 90 minutes).[7] Each has informed this chapter and we thank everyone involved in London and in Denver for their participation and for their continuing inspiration.

In concluding this prompt, we want to consider the themes of falling and failing with which this chapter engages. If using our disciplinary knowledge to reach different audiences is a bit of a stretch, then leaping in, or across, disciplines and practices risks falling between them, as we have already said. We may make a mistake, or miss a step. Falling is closely related to failure – conceptually, culturally, actually. Both falling and failing involve trauma, blows to the body as well as to the mind. But they might also offer opportunities for new work and innovation, tragedy as well as comedy. Falling to fail, as artist and film-maker Tacita Dean has it, carries with it the promise of success. Not to fall, to put it another way, might also entail failure.[8]

In her own comments on falling, Dean was thinking both of the classical myth of Icarus and of the modern artist Bas Jan Ader, who disappeared in 1975 attempting to sail across the Atlantic in the smallest-ever boat. Ader conceived the work as the second part of a triptych, *In Search of the Miraculous*, that was never completed.[9] Did he fall in search of a miracle? In the classical tradition of overreaching and falling, Ovid's Icarus is paradigmatic. Like Dean, Sharon Morris associated falling with Icarus in our first workshop on audience in London, although she had in mind Pieter Bruegel the Elder's *Landscape with the Fall of Icarus* (c. 1555). We take up her prompt here. In this famous painting, the mythological Icarus is not the centre of attention. Rather, he is overlooked, ignored. We have to look hard to find Icarus in Bruegel's modern landscape, and, once we have, we see that he is identifiable only by the evidence of splashes of the blue sea and his two legs.[10] Time is similarly disjointed. There is no harmonious equilibrium between this fallen figure of the mythological past and the Flemish sixteenth-century present. Once you fall for it yourself, you see that this is now a fall complex, poignant and hilarious.

Upside down, Icarus is, as late medieval English would have it, 'up-so-doun'. He fails to fly and falls instead into the sea, while in Bruegel's picture life goes on regardless. The Christian tradition in the medieval West offers us two other falls; the human, that of Adam and Eve, and the angelic, that of the angel Lucifer, who rebels and falls before them and is renamed Satan in consequence. Lucifer falls from the skies into eternity but in their fall Adam and Eve walk out of Eden into time and mortality. Kreider + O'Leary, a collaboration between writer and artist Kristen Kreider and architect James O'Leary, note that this 'is the story of original sin and a fall from grace into knowledge, an apparent correlation between human will and the natural laws of gravity'.[11] Their short book *Falling* opens with a creative-critical account of one of the most famous images of the twentieth century – the first man to walk on the moon – and considers those not in the picture, watching on earth to see whether he will stumble, misstep or even fall. *Falling* then briefly considers Icarus and this moment when 'sky opened up into space' before going on to Newton's discovery of gravity and his falling apple.[12] Falling is both knowledge and activity, Kreider + O'Leary point out. As Tacita Dean, Bas Jan Ader, Pieter Bruegel the Elder and Ovid also teach us, falling is involved in the making of art and of culture and in its downfall. As the story of the Fall of Troy and the tragic falling of the Twin Towers of the World Trade Center in New York instruct, cities and towers fall too. Falling or failing, either way, these are subjects requiring a hearing or an audience.

Three responses on falling

We put our prompt about audience into contemporary medieval practice with three responses. Our first turns on three words and their histories: audience, hearing and falling. Our third returns to word-histories to explore how we might become each other's audience through a heightened awareness of the art of talking, of exchanging our words – conversation. To say that we fall into conversation is a cliché and its metaphor of falling mostly inactive, or dead, however. To reactivate this metaphor for the third response, our second response offers three examples of falling from medieval and modern culture: first, the poem 'Fall' by Sharon Morris from *Gospel Oak*, 2013, second, the reworking and staging of the late medieval morality play *Everyman* in 2015 by poet and writer Carol Ann Duffy for the National Theatre in London, and, third, an early medieval depiction of the Fall of the Angels from the tenth-century Junius manuscript of early English poetry (Oxford, Bodleian Library MS Junius 11, p. 3).[13] These three studies of falling across time – poetic, dramatic, visual – are all informed by acts of translation. The first poem in Morris's *Gospel Oak*, 'Fall', begins by citing the Old English verb 'feallan', 'to fall': the poem itself, rooted in Gospel Oak, an area of North London close to Hampstead Heath, works across time and through the season of fall, autumn. Carol Ann Duffy's *Everyman* is a modern 'adaptation' of the late medieval English play, a devotional allegory that stages a reckoning of the self (or 'everyman') before death and poses the question of how a person might be saved.[14] Time is up for Everyman and a reckoning or accounting before God is in order. Duffy's twenty-first-century adaptation opens with the character of Everyman's slow and literal descent to the stage, an image uncannily similar to the opening credits of the American TV series *Mad Men*, and a subtle allusion, perhaps, to the acts of falling performed by the artist Bas Jan Ader (see Figure 3.1).[15] The script of Duffy's adaptation stresses that most of the play takes place as Everyman falls from his balcony to his death. In free fall (Duffy, *Everyman*, 11).

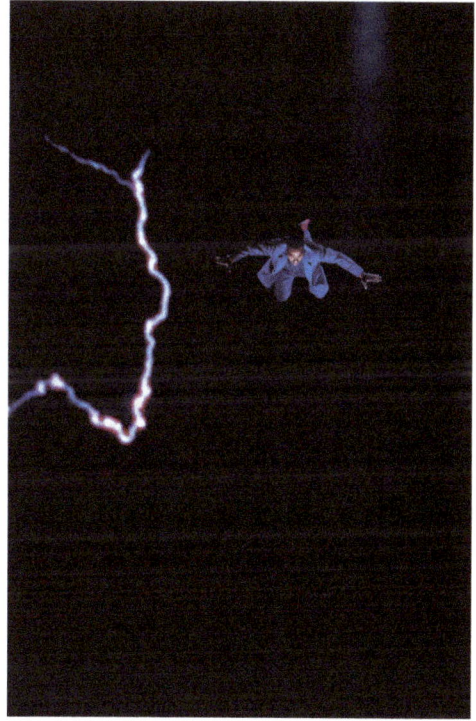

Figure 3.1   Chiwetel Ejiofor in *Everyman*, National Theatre, 2015. Photo © Richard Hubert Smith.

Every man falls, the Christian tradition argues, but the angels fell first. The pictorial image and related poetic accounts of the fall of the angels in the early medieval Junius manuscript adapt and translate this scene into early English culture. The depiction of the falling angels finds an analogue in the slightly later *Old English Hexateuch* (London, British Library, Cotton MS Claudius B iv), while the two poetic narratives known as *Genesis A* and *Genesis B*, with which this image is connected, derive from the scriptural Genesis and from an Old Saxon version of it known as *The Heliand*.[16] The relevant section of the first poem, *Genesis A*, the account of the fall of the angels from the second, *Genesis B* (found in a later section of the manuscript), and the pictorial image of angels falling are in unsettled conversation, with their relationships not entirely clear (see Figure 3.2). On page 2 of the Junius manuscript we find lines 33–48

Figure 3.2 'The Fall of the Angels', Oxford, Bodleian Library MS Junius 11, p. 3. Photo © Bodleian Libraries, University of Oxford.

of *Genesis A*. The full-page image of the fall of the angels on page 3 reads from top to bottom, and is divided into three panels or registers.[17] The visual narrative of the angelic fall is centred on its protagonists: Lucifer on the verge of setting up his rival kingdom in heaven in the top panel, Jesus as the divine incarnate in the middle armed with three arrows directed at Satan below, who is firmly in hell-mouth at the bottom. In this lowest panel, the wings of the fallen angels are clipped, their bodies twisted, turning and tumbling, although the angel who has fallen the most, the outsized Satan, is pinned and chained. We follow – and imagine – this downfall of Lucifer and his transformation into Satan from the top of the page to the bottom, and we are invited to find our own place in Christian salvation history in relation to it.[18] And if we do, we find that we are not in free fall, as in Duffy's *Everyman*; we have already fallen.

The three examples of falling by Sharon Morris, Carol Ann Duffy and the anonymous poet and artist of the Junius manuscript engage poetic, dramatic and visual culture to offer us ideas about audiences for the contemporary medieval that are cross-temporal, cultural, performative and creative. As a collection, *Gospel Oak* charts an archaeology of a place, Gospel Oak, through changing times and seasons, environments (both rural and urban) and histories (both linguistic and cultural). The collection begins with 'Fall', the season of falling leaves, viewed from these different perspectives. Here as elsewhere in Morris's practice, place and environment, word and image, are closely connected. *The Moon is Shining on My Mother* (2017), for example, works the languages of Welsh and English into poetry and into photographic images inspired, in part, by the rich medieval culture of Wales and medieval practices of macaronic poetry. Hers is a contemporary arts practice into which thinking about the medieval and thinking about the environment are firmly embedded.[19]

Duffy's *Everyman* also channels ecological concerns into its modern drama of a fallen, or rather falling, world. Everyone has trashed the planet, a storm rages within and without the figure of Everyman, and the Weather Reporters announce earthquakes and tsunamis (Duffy, *Everyman*, 43–4). As Everyman puts it, 'My parents used to watch the News / and then the Weather. / I saw the Weather turn into the fucking News' (*Everyman*, 44). We explore further the connections between the weather, the news and the self in Chapter 4. Carol Ann Duffy, born in Scotland and Poet Laureate of the United Kingdom from 2009 to 2019, is better known for her poetry than for her plays. The title poem of her first poetry collection in 1985, 'Standing Female Nude', offered us a monologue, a response, if you will, to the gaze of the male artist by the unidentified female model he depicts.[20] The poem sets the stage for Duffy's later work inverting the roles of female muse or object and male artist or subject. In *Everyman*, the character of God/Good Deeds is female, though little is made of this in the play script. The production of *Everyman*, however, makes it clear that bodies, genders and sexualities are all in play in this morality tale. In the modern *Everyman*, every man is up for religious, social and ethical scrutiny from the perspective of God/Good Deeds. Bodies and sexualities are similarly at stake in the anonymously authored Old English Junius poems derived from Genesis. In the scriptural Genesis, the fall of Adam and Eve occasions the introduction of the awareness of the human body and sexual difference into the temporal world, into time.

As the Old English *Genesis* poems and the modern and medieval versions of *Everyman* indicate, therefore, there is a long history of bodies falling in and out of time and place, falling 'in love / or into hell', as Sharon Morris's poem puts it ('Fall', 11). Prompted by Morris's attention to the historic forms of language in *Gospel Oak*, we first reflect on the word-histories for 'audience', 'hearing' and 'falling'. These etymologies too point to the importance of the body and the senses in any understanding of audience.

Response 1: Audience, hearing and falling

As the *Oxford English Dictionary* teaches us, the noun 'audience', derived partly from the Latin noun 'audientia' ('audience', 'listeners') and verb 'audire' ('to hear'), and partly from the French 'audience' (with similar meanings to the Latin), enters the English language in the late fourteenth–early fifteenth century.[21] Its modern meanings of a body or assembly of spectators or listeners, a hearing or a readership are also well attested from the later Middle Ages on. To hold or to be granted an audience or to deliver a speech or discourse to an audience carries associations of presence, social and juridical obligation, as well as the sensory and cognitive actions of listening and hearing, attending and reading. Central to our conception of the contemporary medieval in practice now is our understanding of these long-established meanings of listening to or viewing attentively, of being present to one another, and of forming audiences, communities, bodies of readers for one another.

For those of us who work on early medieval British literary culture, however, evidence for historical audiences is in short supply and often hard to identify. Our understanding of such audiences is often reached through a process of reconstruction and extrapolation from the few literary examples of audiences that have survived.[22] And yet, as all early medievalists know, literary culture in this period of transitional orality was profoundly social and communal, however stratified were these societies in regulating access to knowledge and power. The noun 'audience' derives from later medieval English, as we have seen. For the earlier medieval period, the Old English verbs 'hyran' ('to hear'), and 'hlystan' ('to listen') suggest a range of meanings similar to the modern English usage for 'audience', from hearing or perceiving sound, or a person saying something, to listening attentively or hearkening. What the earliest English vernacular brings out in contrast to contemporary, modern meanings of 'audience', though, is an element of subjection, obedience and explicit teaching or learning from. Old English 'hyran' and 'hlystan' complement a range of Latin equivalents, from the more common – and already mentioned – 'audire', to 'oboedire' ('to obey'), 'ministrare' ('to attend to'), and 'servire' ('to serve').[23] Early medieval English uses include not simply hearing and listening, therefore, but the more particular meanings of listening to a religious service, serving or belonging to a person or group, obeying authority and learning by hearing or being told about. 'Audience' in the early medieval period involves – and in some cases, requires – compulsion and obligation. Taken together, the earliest English meanings of 'audience' have more to do with hearing and attending, as opposed to viewing or spectatorship, than do their modern equivalents. In giving 'audience' a hearing, therefore, those interested in the contemporary medieval need to attend to the hearing and the listening as well as the seeing and the viewing.

Early medievalists, however, are not accustomed to consider modern audiences of our work in any sustained, practical or theoretical way, although we are increasingly aware of the implication of the history of our discipline and its engagement with histories of race and ethnicity, class and gender for modern, contemporary critical practice.[24] This chapter argues that the contemporary medieval offers a way to reflect on our modern as well as medieval audiences and, aware of the risks of interdisciplinary overreach noted earlier, we have chosen 'falling' as our subject.

In Old English as in Modern English, 'feallan' ('to fall') is a very common verb, with literal as well as metaphorical meanings.[25] In both Old and Modern English, we may fall down, through or into; we fall asleep, on our swords, or dead. We may also fall to our knees, subject or prostrate ourselves, particularly in rituals such as prayer. The Toronto *Dictionary of Old English* puts the fall of Lucifer in the class of animate beings who fall, like Adam and Eve, bringing out both physical and moral dimensions of falling.[26] In historic and modern English we may also fall on, over or upon things in both concrete and abstract senses, although there is no attested example of falling in love in Old English, oddly enough. In Old and Modern English, however, things may befall us or fall away. And, as in Modern English, inanimate things fall in Old English as well: rain, snow, water, for example.

Bodies form audiences, these word-histories teach us. We listen and hear, view and attend to those who would have us in their audience – or we might not. Audiences can fall, in terms of numbers (of bodies). Bodies both fail and fall. Falling is an expression of physical embodiment and, as we have seen, of ourselves, our words and our worlds, our histories and environments, cultures and beliefs.

Response 2: Falling – poetry, performance, image

Sharon Morris's modern British poem 'Fall' exemplifies the entanglement of culture and language, environment and history, evident in the etymologies for falling we explored in our first response. Let's take some time to read it here:

FALL
> *feallan, fallanan, -phol-*
>> not a question of morality,
>>> choice or control,
>> that incendiary burn out of summer,
> flames of maple and red pin oak,
>>> sycamore burnt orange;
>> horse chestnut the first to wither, not
>>> through drought or cold
>> but eaten by moths;
> brown leather leaves of English oak
>>> cleave spare to the mast of winter;
>> the City viewed from Hampstead Heath
>>> as though incommensurate.
>> Mouldering leaves.
>> Rotting wood. Decay. Change
>> in the air.
> Acorns, conkers, sweet chestnuts, beech and hazelnuts fall,
>> accumulate the sweet mast
>> of history
>> when pigs and boars rooted for pannage;

seeds split open according to the laws of matter,

                                        utterly familiar

          and yet

          the specifics

          as unpredictable

          as the way we fall in love

          or into hell –

          the forgotten,

          the fallen.

                          (Morris, *Gospel Oak*, p. 11)

The fall of the title of this poem is not a 'question of morality', not the theological Fall, then, or at least not initially. Its subject is autumn, the 'utterly familiar … yet unpredictable' turning of the year as observed on Hampstead Heath with its oaks and maples in the foreground and the City of London in the distance. The use of the noun 'fall' to designate 'autumn' in British English dates from the early modern period, being roughly contemporary with the first recorded reference to the place name of Hampstead Heath, although references to the heath itself as a commons or waste, as it would have been known in the medieval period, date from the tenth century.[27] Morris's ecological philology, her love of words, revives this older usage, later to become standard in American English, synchronizing the history of a place and an environment in this season of autumnal burn-out.

Indeed, 'Fall' lingers on the rich reds and browns of fallen and rotting leaves, naming the acorns, nuts, seeds, or mast which, owing to pannage, allowed the grazing of pigs and boars on common land, whether by legal right or customary privilege. The poem thus anchors fall, autumn, in contemporary and early modern ecologies of the Heath. But the poem's opening word, the startling invocation of the Old English verb 'feallan' ('to fall') in a poem published in 2012, deepens this temporal frame by reaching back into the early medieval period. And its second and third words, 'fallanan', and '-phol-', deepen it further by invoking the apparent origins or roots of 'to fall' and 'fall' in Proto-Germanic and Indo-European respectively.[28] In a poem where words are rooted like trees, 'Fall' restores to the contemporary perspective of the Heath and the City the forgotten words and histories of London's ecological past.

Whether as subjects or readers, human histories are similarly incorporated into the poem's 'laws of matter', even if this is not immediately evident in its opening assertion about the changing seasons ('not a question of morality / choice or control'). Morris's use of white space and lineation on the page draws our eyes across it, from left to right, and then down, in various increments, to its final two lines. These, the last of three groups of lines centred on the page, focus our attention on the central themes of the poem: 'the forgotten, / the fallen'. The 'specifics' of each seasonal fall, the poem argues, are as 'unpredictable' as falling in love or, more provocatively perhaps in this apparently post-Christian poem, 'into hell'. The human condition, our capacity to fall in love or into hell, expresses a world that is changing, falling. Have we forgotten that we are of the world and fall like the leaves with it? Or perhaps fail with it, given the reference to those dying, fallen horse chestnuts, eaten by a new species of bacterium that has destroyed the trees in Europe over the last couple of decades.[29]

'Fall' uses such deep ecologies to maintain a delicate balance between the radically local (Hampstead Heath) and the firmly metropolitan (the City of London), the historical and the contemporary, the forgotten and the fallen, the human and the world. The poem celebrates the last blaze of summer. It is haunted by the English literary tradition of the autumnal poem (Keats's ode, 'To Autumn', comes to mind), but asks of it new questions. What in the world is worthy of the love or the hell into which we might fall in this season of falling leaves, forgotten words and dying trees? 'Fall' is a modern medieval poem to be heard and seen, drawing on both visual and verbal codes for poetic representation. In giving 'Fall' a hearing and an audience, therefore, Morris asks us to consider ecological philology as a form of ethical poetic practice.

We hear Morris's poem as it falls through time and across language, and see this movement as we read the poem on the page. Seeing falling, and visualizing its layered cultural, environmental and religious associations and our ethical response to these effects, are where we move next. We take up the idea of the Fall in Carol Ann Duffy's play *Everyman* to focus on its visualization in the opening scene of the National Theatre production, and we also consider the opening credits of the TV series *Mad Men*.[30] Two men are falling. One is black British, one white American.

In Duffy's play, the fall of her contemporary Everyman, played by Chiwetel Ejiofor (a British actor of Nigerian descent), is a fall to earth not hell, and hell is visualized as its secular counterpart, hell on earth. This brand of hell is imaged in the opening scene, and throughout the play, via the nightmarish excesses and austerity of post-2008 Britain, and a continual barrage of audio-visual reminders of these. Theatre critic Natasha Tripney describes it thus: 'As entrances go it's quite something. Chiwetel

Ejiofor's Everyman is first seen tumbling from above, descending slowly to earth by way of wires, flailing against a backdrop of flickering video'.[31] When Everyman arrives, hits bottom, as it were, in this opening scene, he falls face down and is aware of his own descent. This slow descent to the stage, and the obvious theatricality of the harness that suspends him, hold the idea of free fall in check. Duffy's Everyman sees what's coming. The end of his physical fall becomes the beginning of his passage through this secular brand of hell, and his possible redemption: in this modern instance it will be his relocation in this world. Duffy radically resituates the medieval play's conception of God, hell, religion and spirituality. While her contemporary Everyman hesitantly repeats to himself 'I think I have a soul' at the end of Duffy's play, the character of God/Good Deeds – a woman, remember – comments that 'Religion is a man-made thing. It too will pass ... ' (Duffy, *Everyman*, 64–5).

The figure in the *Mad Men* credits, white American actor Jon Hamm, who plays Don Draper, a Madison Avenue advertising executive in the 1960s, tumbles randomly; he is, initially anyway, in free fall, suggesting suicidal abandon. He falls alongside a skyscraper, which measures stages, or passages, during another fall to earth-not-hell/earth-as-hell, passing by and through images of both material excess and family containment. He falls through his own life. This figure, however, lands on his feet, or, rather, comfortably ensconced on a couch, smoking a cigarette. Is this flight, fall or continued transit? Or a case of arrested development?

We don't claim that the American series specifically adopts this most medieval of preoccupations, the Fall, or that it parallels Carol Ann Duffy's self-conscious and deliberate engagement with the medieval. Matthew Weiner, the creator of the *Mad Men* series, has described this opening 'fall' as that of any American businessman: 'the origin of the credits was I had an idea about a guy getting up in the morning – a faceless man, not even Don, I didn't know who he was – going to work and going in, walking past the office, going into his office, opening the window and jumping out'.[32] The jump and fall are everyday ordinary occurrences, Weiner insists, and are not meant to resonate with contemporaneous images like that of the man falling from the World Trade Center on 9/11, or with any iconic associations, medieval or otherwise. However, as we point out below, the 9/11 image is hard to eradicate from our contemporary collective memory, and critics have suggested that Don Draper's progress within the series does resemble Dante's long walk to hell.[33] We can legitimately ask whether the 'Fall' of Carol Ann Duffy's black British Everyman is resourcing the modern through the medieval, breaking with the medieval, or whether her play is transformative engagement. But what about that other falling, white American, businessman? There is more to be said about the moral, racial and gendered implications of these two modern journeys, and their entanglement with the medieval, however much we simply concentrate on these two visual scenes of falling. We are responsible for bringing these far from universal 'everymen' together – disparate as they are, specified by race and nation, and each pinned within a decade-specific time-frame. Does their extreme difference preclude or embrace – make possible – an encounter with the medieval? Included in these points of contact for a modern audience are assumptions about race as well as history. Is a British Nigerian 'everyman' a universalizing gesture or does it signify that this racial category stands, as ever, for all fallen black men? Does this white American man speak to an imbrication of masculinity and capitalism as well as to white privilege and fragility? Our perspectives as critical contemporary medievalists point to the complexities of ideas of the fallen in the contemporary as well as the medieval worlds.

Our final example of falling is also our earliest, the image of the fall of the angels from the tenth-century manuscript of Old English poetry, the Junius manuscript, p. 3.

Its particularity as a pictorial image from the tenth century risks alienating modern audiences unfamiliar with its representational conventions, although the graphic quality of the page's three registers or panels might be a place where the early medieval and the modern begin to converge.[34] In much the same way, the image's subject of Lucifer's fall from heaven into the mouth of hell speaks more to the theological and poetic concerns of its time than to more modern ones, although Duffy's *Everyman* might give us pause for thought. Modern forms of falling – the drama of *Everyman*, the poetry of Morris's 'Fall' – also help alert us to the pictorial creativity and invention at work in this early medieval image. We are not the first to make this connection. Discussing the aesthetics of falling, Asa Mittman and Susan Kim point to the famous and traumatic photograph of *The Falling Man, September 11, 2001* by Richard Drew.[35] This is an image of an event that rightly haunts any contemporary discussion of falling, initiating for many a temporal rift – before 9/11 and after it. And, indeed, it formed a topic of conversation in both of our workshops. These medieval and modern images of falling, unlike in so many other ways, as Mittman and Kim note, address what we might share when we fall: our fears, our fragility and our humanity.

We have already seen how the depiction of the falling angels offsets the Old English poetic narrative, *Genesis A*, which both precedes and follows it in the Junius manuscript, as well as the account of the fall of the angels known as *Genesis B* later in this same manuscript. Like the visual image, the poems are inventions as well as translations, further alerting us to the creativity at work here. *Genesis A* and *Genesis B* combine to form a single poetic narrative in the Junius manuscript and rework scriptural and Old High German accounts of Genesis respectively, as we noted earlier. But these are also early English poems, condensed, unique poetic histories that make use of Old English conventions, secular as well as sacred.[36] Understanding the theology of the Fall, of Adam and Eve as well as the fall of the angels, was a going cultural concern in the tenth century, and, in order to explore that concern, poets and artists alike had to invent. Scripture offered no clear narrative about the falling of Lucifer and the angels, and representational models were few. This makes the image of the fall of the angels on page 3 of the Junius manuscript all the more remarkable.

In their detailed analysis of the Junius fall, Mittman and Kim draw attention to the representational problem presented by the transformation of the angel, Lucifer, into the fallen devil, Satan. The Junius image shows the angelic Lucifer in heaven and the satanic devil in hell-mouth in the first and third of the registers or panels of the picture. We do not see, however, the angel shape-shifting into Satan, although at the top of the third panel (which is in effect divided into two), we see what looks like a distinctly human-shaped Lucifer, folded over the entrance to hell. This figure is a counterpoint for the much larger, dominant image of the demonic Satan directly beneath it, surrounded by the fallen angels tumbling into hell. Satan is chained and immobile but hell is groundless – there is no frame to this lowest panel.[37] As already noted, the Junius image engages our looking from top to bottom; the early medieval audience viewed the fall of the angels in the light of their own fallen nature. Lucifer, depicted as folded over threshold to hell, part-human, part-angel, focuses this identification.

Satan too shares human features, however demonized. His figure is the largest and most compelling of all the Junius figures. His hair is outlined in flaming red, and his skin is darkened and draws on an early medieval skin-scape of darkness and blackness in contrast to those who fall around him.[38] The image, then, re-engages the politics of race discussed with reference to Duffy's black British *Everyman*, in this case drawing on representational conventions not just for the demonic reversal of the light-bearing and radiant Lucifer but on those of, for example, the roughly contemporary Ethiopians from the early medieval tradition of wonders and marvels. Satan is part-human, part-demon, and the image focuses this identification too. The audience for this image is asked, then, to imagine being in the middle, part-divine, part-demonic, already fallen. We hear echoes of Duffy's Everyman wondering to himself, 'I think I have a soul' (Duffy, *Everyman*, 64).

Response 3: Falling into conversation ... and a conclusion

Our first and second responses have suggested a relationship between our subjects of audience and of falling. In this third response we ask how might we now fall into conversation and become one another's audience? What creative or critical practices might deepen our exploration of the audiences for the contemporary medieval?

Prompted by the word-histories for 'audience' and 'falling', the origins of the noun 'conversation' is a place to start. Like 'audience', 'conversation' enters English in the later Middle Ages, first in senses now obsolete and only later, in the early modern period, in the more familiar modern sense of engaging someone in speech. The *Oxford English Dictionary* notes that in the fourteenth century 'conversation', derived from Latin via French, referred to 'the action of living, or having one's being in a place or among persons', or 'figuratively', to 'one's spiritual being', and also to dealing with others, living together, and to conduct, social as well as spiritual bearing, or behaviour in the world.[39] A conversation in the Middle Ages required at least one other person (no talking to yourself, then), and also an awareness of community and place, whether social or spiritual. We might begin by restoring these medieval senses of community and ethical behaviour to current meanings of 'conversation'.

Conversations can also happen to us, befall us. Happenstance, talk by chance, is one pleasure of falling into conversation. However, falling entails risk, as we have seen; our words may fail us, our talk fall silent. This particular association of falling with conversing is where the risks of putting the audience into practice and talking about it are most evident, as Donna Beth Ellard noted in our workshop on audience in Denver. As we saw earlier, audiences can fall; our conversation can fail to be understood. We noted too, however, that falling – and failing – can also lead to something new, to creativity. In Modern English we make conversation – as well as meanings – and we can use this emphasis on making to restore creativity to the practice of conversing with an audience. And, conversely, there are benefits to be had from falling silent. In many activities – poetry readings, theatre, the classroom – silence is often required of an audience and, as we pointed out at the beginning of this chapter, silence is an aid to reflective meditation and learning. In silence as in speaking, things may fall into place.

'Conversation', as its origins in French and Latin in the fourteenth century indicate, is not derived from Old English, but the principle, and its execution, are singularly embedded in this earlier language. The Old English verb 'wrixlan' ('to change, vary, reciprocate') is paired with speaking: in *Beowulf* the phrase 'wordum wrixlan' ('to exchange words') can describe both an introductory conversation between Beowulf and King Hrothgar and the poetic art of storytelling when Hrothgar's court poet entertains the audience in the mead hall after the hero has defeated Grendel (*Beowulf*, lines 366, 874). Poetry too, then, is public conversation with a communal audience. Early English literary culture valued particularly the sense of exchanging words. The Old English riddles, which we discuss in the next chapter, actively engage, indeed demand, a reciprocal audience of listeners or readers, and take the principle of exchange into the domain of word-play.

The ideas of audience and of the presence of an audience make the contemporary medieval present in turn, bringing us into conversation with the past. Practices of contemplation, meditation and conversation are shared by the medieval and modern, contemporary worlds. In our workshops, we asked participants to engage in shared exercises of reading and listening, reflecting and responding, asking them to be each other's audience. The stages of the exercise, we eventually informed those who had not already guessed, are simply a version of those of *Lectio divina* ('divine reading'), a contemplative practice common in monasteries by the time of St Benedict in the sixth century.[40] A key difference is that whereas the monastic practice was originally intended to be solitary, we made this either a one-to-one or a group exercise, extending our idea of audience in conversation with the past. We wondered how we could make use of the depth of concentration and reflection, which is the goal of the solitary practice, and put our audience into practice. Can we translate *Lectio divina* into a more communal and reciprocal form of listening and understanding?[41] How might we make ethical use of such practices in understanding our relation to the past in the present? How might such conversations with the past enable us to listen to the present? These questions might be seen as the co-ordinates of an 'epic' conversation, a phrase we borrow from Chiwetel Ejiofor's insight into *Everyman*; we develop them further in the next chapter.[42] Our concluding thoughts here, however, rest with the subject of the audience. Medievalists are increasingly keen to talk across fields, disciplines and practices: understanding our various audiences, this chapter has argued, facilitates that move, or turn, to the contemporary creative and critical humanities.

Notes

1. *The Audience Studies Reader*, ed. Will Brooker and Deborah Jermyn (London: Routledge, 2003), is a useful introduction, although it is focused on contemporary communication and media theory.
2. Jane Rendell offers a condensed and lucid introduction in *Art and Architecture: A Place Between* (London: I. B. Tauris, 2006), 3–6.
3. For the debate See, for example, John Holden, *Cultural Value and the Crisis of Legitimacy: Why Culture Needs a Democratic Mandate* (London: Demos, 2006), Jonathan Bate, ed., *The Public Value of the Humanities* (London: Bloomsbury Academic, 2011) and Rick Rylance, *Literature and the Public Good* (Oxford: Oxford University Press, 2016). For a case study of audience and 'cultural value', see Jonathan Gross and Stephanie Pitts, 'Audiences for the Contemporary Arts: Exploring Varieties of Participation across Art Forms in Birmingham, UK', *Participations: Journal of Audience & Reception Studies* 13.1 (May 2016): 4–23.
4. See, for example, Andrew B. R. Elliott, *Medievalism, Politics and Mass Media: Appropriating the Middle Ages in the Twenty-First Century* (Woodbridge: D. S. Brewer, 2017), and also Paul B. Sturtevant, *The Middle Ages in Popular Imagination: Memory, Film and Medievalism* (London: I. B. Tauris, 2018).
5. Relevant are Carolyn Dinshaw's concept of the amateur in *How Soon is Now? Medieval Texts, Amateur Readers, and the Queerness of Time* (Durham, N.C.: Duke University Press, 2012) and Robert Mills, *Derek Jarman's Medieval Modern* (Cambridge: D. S. Brewer, 2018). See also Catherine A. M. Clarke, ed., *Medieval Cityscapes Today* (Leeds: ARC Humanities Press, 2019).
6. Daniel Donoghue, *How the Anglo-Saxons Read Their Poems* (Philadelphia: University of Pennsylvania Press, 2018), notes that the Anglo-Saxons practised silent reading as well as reading aloud; see also, more generally, Paul Saenger, *Space between Words: The Origins of Silent Reading* (Stanford, Calif.: Stanford University Press, 1997), Sara Maitland, *A Book of Silence* (London: Granta, 2008), and Diarmaid MacCulloch, *Silence: A Christian History* (New York: Viking, 2013).
7. We might connect the practice of workshop with that of the seminar and the fostering of creative and critical thinking that emerged in Germany in the eighteenth century, later taken up by universities; see Caroline Levine, *Forms: Whole, Rhythm, Hierarchy, Network* (Princeton, N.J.: Princeton University Press, 2015), 46–8.
8. Tacita Dean's comments accompanied her own work on falling, *And He Fell into the Sea*, 1996, on the apparent disappearance at sea of British MP John Stonehouse in 1974, and are excerpted in *Failure*, ed. Lisa Le Feuvre, Documents of Contemporary Art (London: Whitechapel Gallery, 2010), 129–30.
9. Jan Verwoert, *Bas Jan Ader: In Search of the Miraculous* (London: Afterall Books, 2006).
10. For image and introduction, see https://www.bl.uk/collection-items/landscape-with-the-fall-of-icarus/. Accessed 28 January 2019.
11. Kristen Kreider and James O'Leary (Kreider + O'Leary), *Falling* (Ventnor, Isle of Wight: Copy Press, 2015), 74.
12. 'Man on the Moon', in *Falling*, 9–22 at p. 11.
13. Sharon Morris, *Gospel Oak* (London: Enitharmon Press, 2013), 11. Reproduced with thanks to Sharon Morris and Enitharmon Press. *Everyman: A New Adaptation*, by Carol Ann Duffy (London: Faber & Faber, 2015), with details of cast and production, 1–2. See also the photograph of the production included in the British Library medieval collection at https://www.bl.uk/collection-items/~/link.aspx?_id=0CC58AB2875241869754AD89209A30EB&_z=z. Accessed 28 December 2018. Leslie Lockett has a good online bibliographical introduction to the Junius manuscript: http://www.oxfordbibliographies.com/view/document/obo-9780195396584/obo-9780195396584-0145.xml. Accessed 28 December 2018. See also Lockett's 'An Integrated Re-examination of the Dating of Oxford, Bodleian Library, Junius 11', *Anglo-Saxon England* 31 (2002): 141–73.
14. *Everyman and Medieval Miracle Plays*, ed. A. C. Cawley, new edn (London: J. M. Dent, 1993), 195–225. The play is related to a similar one in Dutch; see *Everyman and Its Dutch Original, Elckerlijc*, ed. Clifford Davidson, Martin W. Walsh and Ton J. Broos (Kalamazoo, Mich.: Medieval Institute Publications, 2007). See also Andrew Hadfield, 'The Summoning of Everyman', in *The Oxford Handbook of Tudor Drama*, ed. Thomas Betteridge and Greg Walker (Oxford: Oxford University Press, 2012): 93–108.

15. Duffy's *Everyman* was first produced in the Olivier Auditorium of the National Theatre, London (29 April, 2015), dir. Rufus Norris; for the opening scene, see https://www.youtube.com/watch?v=la0Zg_0Vc9s. Accessed 26 January 2019. The American television series *Mad Men,* created by Matthew Weiner and produced by Lionsgate Television, premiered on 19 July 2007, on the cable network AMC. For the opening credits see https://www.youtube.com/watch?v=WcRr-Fb5xQo. Accessed 26 January 2019. For Bas Jan Ader's famous films of falling, See, for example, *Fall 1, Los Angeles,* 1970 and *Broken Fall (Organic),* 1971.

16. Asa Simon Mittman and Susan M. Kim, 'Locating the Devil *"Her"* in MS Junius 11', *Gesta* 54.1 (2015): 3–25. There is a second image of the angelic fall on page 16 of the manuscript. See also Catherine E. Karkov, *Text and Picture in Anglo-Saxon England: Narrative Strategies in the Junius 11 Manuscript* (Cambridge: University of Cambridge Press, 2001), 19–100.

17. 'Genesis', in *Old Testament Narratives,* ed. and trans. Daniel Anlezark, Dumbarton Oaks Medieval Library 7 (Cambridge, Mass.: Harvard University Press, 2011), 1–203. Junius 11 may be accessed digitally at https://iiif.bodleian.ox.ac.uk/iiif/viewer/d5e3a9fc-abaa-4649-ae48-be207ce8da15#?c=0&m=0&s=0&cv=6&r=0&xywh=-5830%2C-419%2C16482%2C8355. Accessed 31 January 2019.

18. Karkov, *Text and Picture,* 38–9, 40.

19. Sharon Morris, *The Moon is Shining on My Mother* (London: Glynn Vivian Art Gallery with Enitharmon Editions, 2017). Morris's artworks include photography, installations, film-poems and live performances with projections; she has exhibited in London and Wales, including *Film in Space,* Camden Arts Centre (2013) and *The Moon and a Smile,* Glynn Vivian Art Gallery, Swansea (2017).

20. Carol Ann Duffy, *Standing Female Nude* (London: Anvil Press Poetry, 1985, repr. London: Picador, 2016), 46, 44.

21. 'audience', n.1. *OED Online.* June 2018. Oxford University Press. http://www.oed.com/view/Entry/13022?redirectedFrom=audience. Accessed 19 June 2018.

22. For an introduction see Hugh Magennis, 'Audience(s), Reception, Literacy', in *A Companion to Anglo-Saxon Literature,* ed. Phillip Pulsiano and Elaine Treharne (Oxford: Blackwell Publishing, 2001), 84–101.

23. 'hȳran', vb. and 'hlystan', vb. *The Dictionary of Old English: A to I.* University of Toronto. https://tapor.library.utoronto.ca/doe/. Accessed 19 June 2018.

24. See above, note 4.

25. 'fall', v. *OED Online.* June 2018. Oxford University Press. http://www.oed.com/view/Entry/67829?isAdvanced=false&result=3&rskey=4pCMEq&. Accessed 19 June 2018. See also 'feallan', vb., and 'gefeall', n., 'gefyll', n., *The Dictionary of Old English A to I.* University of Toronto: https://tapor.library.utoronto.ca/doe/. Accessed 19 June 2018.

26. 'feallan', vb., A. i. d. *The Dictionary of Old English: A to I.* University of Toronto: https://tapor.library.utoronto.ca/doe/. Accessed 19 June 2018.

27. 'fall', n.2. VI. *OED Online.* June 2018. Oxford University Press. http://www.oed.com/view/Entry/67826. Accessed 20 June 2018. See also T. F. T. Baker, Diane K. Bolton and Patricia E. C. Croot, 'Hampstead: Settlement and Growth' and 'Hampstead: Hampstead Heath', in *A History of the County of Middlesex: Volume 9, Hampstead, Paddington,* ed. C. R. Elrington (London: Victoria County History, 1989), 8–15, 75–81. *British History Online,* http://www.british-history.ac.uk/vch/middx/vol9/pp75-81 and http://www.british-history.ac.uk/vch/middx/vol9/pp8-15. Accessed 20 June 2018.

28. The etymology of *IE *phol,* like that of Proto-Germanic **fallanan,* is uncertain. See Alfred Bammesberger, 'The Place of English in Germanic and Indo-European', in *The Cambridge History of the English Language. Volume I: The Beginnings to 1066,* ed. Richard M. Hogg (Cambridge: Cambridge University Press, 1992), 26–66, at 35–6.

29. For an introduction to the horse chestnut leaf-miner disease, see Tetsuo Kokubun, 'Horse Chestnut under Attack', https://www.kew.org/read-and-watch/horse-chestnut. Accessed 30 May 2019.

30. *Everyman,* https://www.youtube.com/watch?v=la0Zg_0Vc9s; accessed 26 January 2019; *Mad Men,* https://www.youtube.com/watch?v=WcRr-Fb5xQo. Accessed 26 January 2019.

31. Natasha Tripney, *The Stage,* 30 April 2015. https://www.thestage.co.uk/reviews/2015/everyman-2/. Accessed 20 January 2019.

32. Esther Zuckerman, 'Mad Men Stands at the Window', *The Atlantic,* 21 June, 2013. https://www.theatlantic.com/entertainment/archive/2013/06/mad-men-falling-man-finale/314016/. Accessed 26 January 2019.

33. Zuckerman, 'Mad Men Stands at the Window'. The connection might be made the other way as well: the cover of Thomas Meyer's Beowulf: A Translation (Brooklyn, N.Y.: Punctum Books, 2012) inserts the image of a figure falling between two images of Viking ships.
34. Mittman and Kim make a similar observation: 'Locating the Devil', 24.
35. Mittman and Kim, 'Locating the Devil,' 22–3.
36. Anlezark offers a useful introduction in Old Testament Narratives, vii–xv.
37. Mittman and Kim, 'Locating the Devil.
38. Mittman and Kim, 'Locating the Devil'. More generally, see Geraldine Heng, 'Color', in The Invention of Race in the European Middle Ages (Cambridge: Cambridge University Press, 2018), 181–256.
39. 'conversation', n.. OED Online. June 2018. Oxford University Press. http://www.oed.com/view/Entry/40748?rskey=SctJev&result=1. Accessed 21 June 2018.
40. See Jean Leclercq, Love of Learning and Desire for God: A Study of Monastic Culture, trans. Catharine Misrahi, 3rd edn (New York: Fordham University Press, 1982).
41. For a useful overview of the history and practice of Lectio Divina and its incorporation into modern meditative practices, see https://www.contemplativeoutreach.org/category/category/lectio-divina. Accessed 26 January 2019.
42. For Chiwetel Ejiofor's comments on Everyman, see NT Talks podcast, 'Chiwetel Ejiofor on Everyman', https://player.fm/series/nt-talks/chiwetel-ejiofor-on-everyman. Accessed 30 May 2019.

4
Water: seven propositions for the contemporary medieval

This chapter offers seven propositions – a manifesto in seven parts, if you will – for working with the contemporary medieval. Our seven propositions offer co-ordinates for an 'epic' conversation of the kind we identified in Chapter 3. This time around, however, our conversation has only one subject: water. We first explored the subject of water in Chapter 2 and, because of that, artist Roni Horn's practice of working with and through water. In this chapter, we put Horn's work alongside that of Caroline Bergvall (particularly her multimedia performance and book, *Drift*, of 2014) and the sculptures of Inuvialuit artist Abraham Anghik Ruben. Horn (b. 1955), Ruben (b. 1951) and Bergvall (b. 1962) open up pathways of connection to medieval cultural and literary practice from North American, Inuvialuit and European perspectives. Each artist makes their own distinctive connection with the deep past, which has inspired us, indeed demanded of us new modes of performative, creative scholarship to best elucidate them.[1]

We are inspired by the artwork of Bergvall, Horn and Ruben to suggest a different kind of research about or conversation with the past: one where we can hold medieval and modern in flux and reciprocity, where the past and present source each other, where the medieval and the modern interact, flow, cross and pass. Accordingly, we examine the rivers, oceans and libraries of, for example, the Iceland and England of Roni Horn, the Mediterranean and North Sea of Caroline Bergvall, and the Atlantic passage of Ruben's sculptures about Inuit and Viking memories of travel on the sea. Examining how contemporary creative practices might relate to medieval studies, we use the concept of 'proposition' creatively, rather than formally.

Indeed, exploring water and its environs offers us an instance and mode of practice where we can engage the contemporary medieval creatively and imaginatively. We offer wonder, a process of affective engagement with the past, as an important dimension of our 'epic' conversation across time and space. Where does water belong, we wonder? To what discipline? In this chapter we follow water as it enters Horn's work (Proposition One), as it flows into the past and into the sea and shifts into ice in Exeter Book Riddle 69 (Proposition Two), as it conjures a riddle of the self (Proposition Three), as it morphs into journey, weather and stormy-minded men in *Beowulf* (Proposition Four), as it creates a passage between the past and the present in Ruben's sculpting of voyage, travel and migration between Viking and Inuit cultures (Proposition Five), and as the 'drift' between words and peoples in Caroline Bergvall's multimedia performance and book of the same title, reworking accounts of early medieval journeys such as that imagined in the Old English poem, *The Seafarer* (Propositions Six and Seven). Water and wonder propose a methodology and a practice; water brings with it, inevitably, weather and voyage, and these too merit our critical attention.

Proposition one: Water is a master verb, or, *Still Water,* Roni Horn

And so we return to water, and to Roni Horn and the modern moment in contemporary arts production, to begin our conversation across periods and disciplines, creative and scholarly practices. How might water be said to be a master verb, as our first proposition suggests? And what does the artwork, *Still Water,* by Roni Horn (1999), have to do with it (see Figure 4.1)?[2] After all, Roni Horn is not interested in the medieval period, though she takes water as her subject regularly. She is not at all interested in periodization or chronology, but her practice as sculptor and visual artist profoundly engages with ideas about the fluidity of time and temporality.

And so our first proposition borrows from the title of *Still Water (The Thames, for Example)* of 1999 by Horn, now in the Tate Modern in London. The work is a series of large-scale photographs of the River Thames, each annotated with footnotes that offer points of connection between the artist, the viewer and the image, summoning a range of affective associations, fear and awe included. The flow of the Thames is stilled by the photographs, perhaps, but these images still capture the undulation, depths and texture of this rapidly changing tidal river, conduit for history and culture, and equally well known for its suicides. Still

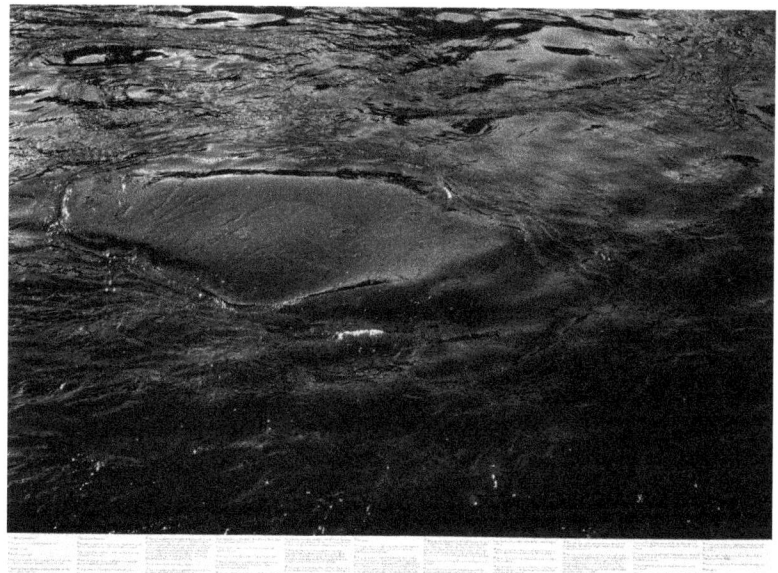

Figure 4.1 Roni Horn, *Still Water (The River Thames, for Example)*, 1999 (detail). Fifteen framed photographs and text printed on uncoated paper, 30.5 × 41.5″ / 77.5 × 105.4 cm each. Photo by Bill Jacobson.

water. The photographs in the series point to the many meanings that this phrase might hold. Water can be still, can be stilled, literally and metaphorically, and can still be our subject, our 'master' verb, as Horn herself notes. Characteristically, Horn's phrase provokes. It poses the question of whether or not water can be gendered and so challenges us to think about mastery as a practice that might move beyond its conventional associations with masculinity and domination – and indeed the human – to something more fluid, transitional and relational. Expertise and expert knowledge come into play here too, as practices never quite mastered and always in flux: there is, after all, always more to be learned.

Whether in whole or in part, Horn has used her self-coined aphorism 'Water is the master verb; an act of perpetual relation', in a number of contexts. It annotates, by way of one footnote among many, her photographic studies in *Still Water (The Thames, for Example)*, for example. It reappears in another installation of this work, the punningly titled *Some Thames*, a permanent installation at the University of Akureyri, Iceland (2000), revisited for the Art Institute of Chicago (2004) (Figures 4.2, 4.3 and 4.4).

Figure 4.2 Roni Horn, *Some Thames*, 2000 (detail). Eighty photographs printed on paper. 25 × 38″ / 63.5 × 96.5 cm each. Photo by Roni Horn.

Figure 4.3 Roni Horn, *Some Thames*, 2000 (detail). Eighty photographs printed on paper. 25 × 38″ / 63.5 × 96.5 cm each. Photo by Roni Horn.

Figure 4.4   Roni Horn, *Some Thames*, 2000 (detail). Eighty photographs printed on paper. 25 × 38″ / 63.5 × 96.5 cm each. Installation view: University of Akureyri, Iceland. Photo by Stefan Altenburger.

Horn quotes herself in her monologue, *Saying Water*.[3] And she offers the same thought as an opportunity for 'annotation' (the word is Horn's) or gloss (this is our annotation) to create a textual conversation, or set of dialogues, in her four-volume artist's book, *Wonderwater (Alice Offshore)* of 2004.[4] As we might expect from this artist who has so often taken water as her subject, Alice in this iteration is not in wonderland, she is offshore, wondering about water.

The four volumes *of Wonderwater* collect responses to Horn's work from artist Louise Bourgeois, poet and classicist Anne Carson, philosopher and gender theorist Hélène Cixous, and, inevitably given his surname, director and film-maker John Waters. Each volume offers responses (or refusals to respond) to Horn's own postulates, descriptions, aphorisms and musings about water. Cixous, for example, starts her response to Horn's 'Water is the master verb' with a single French noun, 'eau', and continues, punningly, 'eau / o au haut en oh' (which we can barely say!). John Waters offers his own, characteristic, spin on the same statement: 'Ethel Waters's relentless struggle to claw her way to the top of all forms of show business' – Ethel Waters, the woman who sang *Stormy Weather* for the first time in the Cotton Club, New York, in 1933.[5] From John

Waters to Ethel Waters to *Stormy Weather*, puns in and across languages, humour (pointed or not), cultural knowledge not necessarily shared by all (who was Ethel Waters, again?), the language play in *Wonderwater* crosses over with, flows into, the kinds of language play enjoyed by early medieval poets, riddle-makers in especial. In these ways, Horn's work offers us a contemporary gloss on medieval practices and a pathway into interpretation.

Indeed, Horn's making and remaking of work in a variety of media, whether on her own or collaboratively, invites us to think – slowly – about rumination, process, repetition, expansion, self-examination and the relation between self and the world. As we pointed out in Chapter 2, we first became interested in Horn because of her interest in Iceland and its watery environment, most notably in the ten-volume series of artist's books *Ísland: To Place*, and in the celebrated installations and books *You Are the Weather, Parts 1 and 2* (1994–7, 2010–11) and *Vatnasafn/Library of Water* (2007) at Stykkishólmur.[6] In 'Women and Water: Icelandic Tales and Anglo-Saxon Moorings' we explored landscape, place and gender as fruitful categories of analysis in relation to some of Horn's work.[7] Here we are now, still engaging with water and with the proposition that water offers us a 'master' verb. And still thinking about the time of water – its relation to temporality and to disciplinarity. Horn's practice makes us wonder about water, and so it challenges us to wonder about it as medievalists. Each encounter with her work has opened up a passage from the modern to the medieval that has expanded and developed our understanding of the riddle of early medieval encounters with water, with selfhood and with being in the world.

Proposition Two: Practising wonder, or, Exeter Book Riddle 69

Early medieval riddles were open to wonder, to wondering about the world, and to engaging with water as one of their subjects. Take this example:

Wundor wearð on wege; wæter wearð to bane.[8]

In Modern English, we might put it this way:

A wonder was on its way – water was as bone

Poet and translator Kevin Crossley-Holland, known for his long-standing engagement with Anglo-Saxon poetry, puts it another:

> On the way a miracle: water become bone.[9]

And so this one-line riddle, Exeter Book Riddle 69, with its solution of 'ice' or 'iceberg', becomes a good way to capture the wonder of water. Water is both liquid and solid, place and substance and, as the translations indicate, medieval and modern; this riddle is about a body of water, a metaphor as resonant now as in the early medieval period. The riddle's alliteration ('wundor', 'wege', 'wæter', 'wearð') and repetition ('wearð') draw sonic and visual attention to that isolated noun 'ban', 'bone'; the boniness of water. Ice. Iceberg. Stilled water. Water, still.

Riddle 69 is one of the great single-line riddles of the vernacular, Old English, corpus of riddles – if, that is, it is a one-liner. Riddle 69 is preceded in the Exeter Book by another couple of lines, identified as Riddle 68 by editors Krapp and Dobbie, and apparently incomplete or unfinished:

> Ic þa wiht geseah   on weg feran;
> heo wæs wrætlice   wundrum gegierwed

We might put it this way:

> I saw a creature travelling on her way; she was artful, marvellously adorned

Some interpreters, such as Craig Williamson, read Riddles 68 and 69 as one:

> Ic þa wiht geseah   on weg feran;
> heo wæs wrætlice   wundrum gegierwed.
> Wundor wearð on wege;   wæter wearð to bane.[10]

And so we might respond:

> I saw a creature travelling on her way;
> She was artful, wonderfully adorned.
> A wonder was on its way –
> water was as bone

In this riddle water now has the shape of a woman. Contemporary American poet Jennifer Grotz, commissioned by *The Word Exchange*, has this:

> I saw that creature wander on the way,
> Wonderfully adorned. A wonder floating on a wave:
> She was water turned to bone[11]

As we work through these possible relations, we realize that this interpretive flexibility is entirely to our point. One riddle or two (Riddle 68 or Riddle 69); singular or multiple, both of form and of forms of translation; human or non-human; a creature wonderfully adorned, dressed appropriately as only elite Anglo-Saxon women are in Old English poetry, ornate, ornamented; artfully adorned; a wonder-woman, perhaps, fluid, like water, still water, icy, like bone, ice, a water-woman.

To which Roni Horn might reply, helpfully, 'Water is the master verb; an act of perpetual relation' (Horn, *Saying Water*).

Proposition Three: The self is a riddle and the riddle is a self

What is a riddle 'about'? Literary interpretation of the Old English riddles points out that they are less 'about' their solutions than about the process of deciphering, imagining or answering the questions they pose.[12] This idea of a conversation in process engages the audience, the listener or the reader in a complicated internalized dialogue in order to puzzle out the riddle: it's me, myself and my shadow, my speaking self, my hearing self, my literate self, my obdurate stupid self who does not get it, my funny self, my gendered self, the self that wonders about Old English and wants to know. Early medieval riddles are creations of artifice and highly self-conscious artefacts. Such self-consciousness cuts both ways, however, as the riddles demand our equally self-conscious creative participation, as we have just seen in our reading of Exeter Book Riddles 68 and 69. When we talk about riddles and the self, then, and about self-consciousness in early medieval England, what is it that we are really talking about? Are we riddling the self? Roni Horn poses a similar question: 'When you talk about water, aren't you really talking about yourself? Isn't water like the weather that way?' (Horn, *Saying Water*).

'Wundor' and its compound adjective 'wundorlic' ('wonder-like') appear in twenty-one of the Old English Exeter Book riddles, though most if not all of the roughly one hundred riddles elicit 'wondering', which is an underlying necessity and touchstone for the riddling mentality. How does one think in, or respond to, the presence of a wonder, a marvel? Who wants to know, how, and how much? Wonder and wondering are closely related to another well-known concept of riddling, invoked by the adjective 'wrætlic', with its meanings of 'splendidly, wondrously, highly wrought', a declaration, if you will, of the wonder embedded in self-conscious artifice. In his examination of wondering as a perceptual frame for the Riddles, Peter Ramey lists a total of fifty instances of these 'wonder words', a high concentration when compared with the Old English corpus.[13] The combined riddle that is Exeter Book Riddles 68 and 69 intertwines the processes of wonder and of artifice, creation and perception, describing a watery creature who 'wæs wrætlice wundrum gegier-wed' ('wrought of, or splendidly adorned with, wonders'), as we saw in Proposition Two.

'Wundor', 'wonder' and, again, water. The relation of water to wonder became itself a riddle when we tried to ask how frequent or how pervasive the idea of water is in the Exeter Book riddles. Some things are easier to count than others, and there are maybe twenty riddles that declare, conjure or are at play with water.[14] In addition to the more obvious riddles that include water or ice as their solutions, such as Riddles 33, 68/69 and 84, what counts? Should we also count Riddle 51, with its solution of 'pen and three fingers', where the 'wrætlic' creature flies high in the air and then plunges down into the waves ('fleag on lyfte, / deaf under yþe')? This riddle creature is a compound image for the physical and material process of writing, as the feathered bird-pen dips and dives into a sea of ink. Should we also count the many other references to weather, wind, storm, anchor, various birds, ships or reed-pens, all of which are related to water in one way or another? Our answer is yes. In the riddles, water is connected to the miraculous, to transformation, to process, to generation and, as we have already seen in the case of Riddle 69, to gender and identity formation. Water is itself wondrous and elicits our sense of wonder, all wonderfully and succinctly expressed in Riddle 69, with its solution of 'ice' or 'iceberg'. In this riddle, ice is described as both 'wundor' and 'wrætlic': the riddle invites us to observe and engage with water's process of becoming ice, but also to engage with the conscious experience of its becoming, entailing cognition (wondering) and aesthetic realization (wonder): 'Wundor wearð on wege; wæter wearð to bane'.

There is a clear general case to be made for the wonder of water in the Old English riddles, then, and so too throughout the literary corpus, as we will see further in the next chapter when we consider a wide range of water words. The connection of wonder and water to the process of identity formation and the riddle of the self is perhaps more opaque. How might we follow the process of a self, or a mind at work, engaging in a multifaceted internalized dialogue with that self in order to puzzle out a riddle? Let's consider briefly Riddle 60, 'reed-pen', which we read as a revolving, circular conversation among a number of possible speaking and hearing selves. The many dimensions of this riddle are all born(e) out of and along by water: reeds, pens, messengers, messages, sender, receiver and, last but not least, the audience, reader or listener.[15] Here is the complete riddle:

> Ic wæs be sonde,   sæwealle neah,
> æt merefaroþe,   minum gewunade
> frumstaþole fæst;   fea ænig wæs
> monna cynnes,   þæt minne þær
> on anæde   eard beheolde,
> ac mec uhtna gehwam   yð sio brune
> lagufæðme beleolc.   Lyt ic wende
> þæt ic ær oþþe sið æfre sceolde
> ofer meodubence muðleas sprecan,
> wordum wrixlan.   Þæt is wundres dæl
> on sefan searolic   þam þe swylc ne conn,
> hu mec seaxes ord   ond seo swiþre hond,
> eorles ingeþonc   ond ord somod
> þingum geþydan,   þæt ic wiþ þe sceolde
> for unc anum twam   ærendspræce
> abeodan bealdlice,   swa hit beorna ma
> uncre wordcwidas   widdor ne mænden.

A literal translation might put it this way:

> I was by the shore, near the sea wall, / at the water's edge I dwelled / fast in my original foundation / there were few / of mankind who there, / in that solitude, could see my home, / but each hour before dawn the dark wave, / surrounded me with a watery embrace. / Little did I expect / ever before or after, / I, across the mead-bench should speak mouthless, / exchange words. It is a share of wonder / to one who does not know such things, / how, with a cunning mind, the point of a knife, / the right hand and the intent of a man together in a point, / join for this reason, that I with you should, / for us two alone a message-speech / boldly declare, so that no men / should spread our word-speeches more widely.

What is this riddle about? It is spoken in the voice of a reed-pen, which as a reed was once firmly anchored in water, 'frumstaþole fæst' (line 3, 'fast in its original foundation' or 'fast-rooted in my first life', as contemporary poet Jane Hirshfield, also commissioned by *The Word Exchange*, has it).[16] The voice of the reed is not heard, however, at least in the conceit of the riddle itself. Nor is it observed by the race or kin of men ('monna cynnes'), save for those of us who comprise the riddle's audience – its auditors or readers, watchers or wonderers.[17] The only presence other than the reed at the beginning of this riddle is the water that surrounds, embraces and observes it at that very *Wanderer* time of day: 'ac mec uhtna gehwam / yð sio brune lagufæðme beleolc' ('but every hour before dawn the dark wave surrounded me with a watery embrace', 6–7).[18] The transformation of the riddle creature as reed into a pen and then voice, utterance, mouthless ('muðleas') speech and written language, is, unsurprisingly, a bit of a wonder ('is wundres dæl', 9). But it is one available to those who wonder, who understand the mystery of the coming together of inanimate objects, the points of a knife and a quill, and animate thought, the 'intent of a man' ('eorles ingeþonc', 12). Although the communicability of language and its ability to travel, its portability, can extend to communal conversation in the form of an exchange of words between two men in the mead hall (this riddle argues), what is at stake here, finally, is a message about an internalized conversation to which no-one else is privy. This mouthless, silent, private inter-subjectivity is not shared in the form of a message whose contents we can decipher, even though there may be many literate listeners and readers who share the 'wonder' of the riddling language that can describe this kind of silent communication.

Indeed, the riddle circles back on itself, to its beginning, to the silence and solitude that water and reed and speaker and listener, and only these, now share: 'that I with you should for us two alone a message-speech boldly declare, so that no men should spread our word-speeches more widely'. Our inelegant translation emphasizes the idea of conversation, then, but an internal, stilled one. But whether the exchange is internal or communally directed, we can see that this 'exchange of words' ('wordum wrixlan'), the same phrase with which we concluded our discussion of audience and/in conversation in Chapter 3, is still part of our larger conversation with the past. To hear the water-born(e) voice of the reed-as-pen is also to see oneself as reader, and to speak silently to oneself, interpreting its message of silent speech as known only to those for whom it is intended. Figuring out the movement and process of the riddle, and not necessarily its answer, is a conversation with and revelation of self and its relation to language. As the riddle ends, the doubled perspectives of speaker and listener are bound, coalesced, in a silent shared understanding of the power and paradox that is written language. And this paradox redoubles, if we assume that it was shared, read aloud, performed.

We cannot finally untangle this paradox, even if we satisfactorily nail down the 'answer' to the riddle. We continue to wonder about it. Indeed, in the process of translating it, and trying to grapple as closely as we could with the asymmetries and vagaries of Old English grammatical structure, we had many discussions about how, and not what, it means. We also wondered whether to include any other less literal and more user-friendly translations, of which there are many, and settled on this one by Craig Williamson:

> Rooted near water, raised by the shore,
> I was earth-fast, bound in a bed,
> My native land. Few men walked
> In this wilderness, watched as the wave
> Played round my body with its dark arms
> At dusk and dawn. I did not dream
> That someday I should speak, slip words
> Over benches, mouthless in the mead-hall.
> That is a miracle to men who do not know
> This craft – how the point of a knife,
> A skilled right hand and a man's intent
> Tooling together should shape me so
> That boldly I bring you my message,
> Singing in silence so no man in the wider
> World may share our words and understand.[19]

Discussing the nuanced differences between these two, or any two, translations will in some measure continue the riddling process, and keep us wondering, keep us in conversation with the past. We leave you, as readers and interpreters yourselves, to ponder our version and Williamson's, and note for good measure a third translation by Jane Hirshfield.[20] In doing so, we anticipate the broader arguments of our final chapter, where we take up the idea of translation, of being in translation in its broadest sense, as both transformation and communication.

It turns out therefore that Riddle 60 is about the many ways we may talk among our selves, and listen to one another. When we talk about riddles of the self and of self-consciousness in early medieval England, aren't we really talking about the relation of the self to the world, written or spoken? And so we return also to Roni Horn's question, 'When you talk about water, aren't you really talking about yourself? Isn't water like the weather that way?' (Horn, *Saying Water*).

Proposition Four: Water is like the weather is like the self

The Old English riddles demonstrate that the semantic world of water is gloriously complicated; it is a perpetual act of relation that is always multiple, plural, in Horn's words. Water is in an act of relation to ice in Riddle 69, for example, while the watery environment of a reed is in relation to a pen and a meditation on writing and communication in Riddle 60. We saw something similar in Chapter 2 in our discussion of the phrase 'cup of the waves' in *Beowulf* ('ȳða ful', line 1208), with its fluid mix of metaphors evoking the feminine, the heroic, the ideas of both motion and containment, and the connective and disjunctive presence of water.[21] A cup can be carried by a queen, it can travel across the sea, and it can be an image of travel, motion, itself. Motion or commotion. Another pathway into or across water is offered by a compound adjective, again from *Beowulf*, 'hrēoh-mōd' (lines 2132, 2581), which we mentioned briefly in Chapter 2 and return to here. To puzzle out the meaning of this adjective is something of an iceberg of research that takes us into the weather and the environment, weather as environment, environment and affect, and the self. It seems that everyone is talking about emotions these days, or affect, or feeling or the weather, whether in scholarship or in everyday life.[22] In England, we often assume that the polite way to avoid talking about anything remotely personal is to talk about the weather, but, to come back to American Roni Horn and her refrain that resonates throughout this chapter, 'Isn't talking about the weather talking about yourself? When you talk about water, aren't you really talking about yourself? Isn't water like the weather that way?' (Horn, *Saying Water*).

So, what does an adjective like 'hrēoh-mōd' and the warrior men who suffer from it in Old English poetry say about the weather, water and the self in the early medieval period? The first part of the compound, 'hrēoh', refers to weather; it means storm, harsh rough elemental forces of all kinds, not necessarily just wet or cold. For every dictionary entry for 'hrēoh' and its compounds, however, there are parallel evocations of emotional states. A storm is a troubled time for warriors on many fronts, where it is connected to physical and emotional pain, upheaval and disturbance. 'Hrēoh' is connected to, or crosses over with, the adjective '(h) reow', 'fierce, turbulent, cruel, distraught, wild, savage'; it is also connected to the noun 'hreow', 'sorrow, grief, regret, remorse, repentance', and to the verb 'hreowan', 'to rue or regret, excite compassion or pity'. And so it goes with the language of Old English – semantic worlds intersect and merge, creating contours of similarity and difference. The other half of the compound, 'mod', is one of the most familiar and widespread terms in Old English, and also, to our thinking, one of the most mysterious in that its semantic field crosses over a variety of affective and abstract categories. It can evoke and pertain to mood, mind, heart, spirit, courage, imagination, and then can become further complicated by its appearance in many compounds. In the Old English poem *The Battle of Maldon*, for example, defeat of the Anglo-Saxons at the hands of the Vikings is put down in part to the 'ofermod' of Byrhtnoth.[23] Having too much 'mod' is problematic, therefore, especially for men, but so is not having enough. Like 'the right stuff', 'mod' can evade precise definition, though 'ego' has proven a useful working translation. Our present point about the compound 'hreoh-mod', and there are many similar ones in Old English, which we look at in the next chapter, is that it suggests a vital relation between self and the world.

Following the intersecting semantic pathways of words like 'hreoh-mod' in Old English poetry causes us to wonder a bit more about warrior men and their world of water, storms, waves and the weather. It also prompts us to wonder more generally about other contours of meaning, and to imagine a relation between self and world in which processes of cross-identification might be imagined as the curving lines of both dissolution and separation on weather maps, those isobars and isotherms that swirl across zones of atmospheric pressure and temperature, showing a temporary – and fictional – static map of the weather of our world. Using weather maps as our image, we wonder about a parallel comprehension of affect, via mind, in connection with body, and in dynamic relation with cultural and physical worlds. In this case, the contours on our map mediate embodiment in relation to environment and fully engage the world as weather, as the Old English word 'hreoh-mod' suggests. Warriors and storms. If *You Are the Weather*, as the title of Horn's series of photographs of the same woman emerging from, or immersed in, various hot springs and pools in Iceland suggests, then *Weather Reports You*, as Horn's title for the community narratives about the weather installed at the *Library of Water* indicates. The contoured lines on our weather maps of the body and the world hold and dissolve, demarcate but do not define. They are always going both ways.

Proposition Five: Time is travel, or, seafaring

Storms and the voyages of men, inner and outer, lead us to introduce into our epic conversation about the medieval and the modern the work of Inuvialuit sculptor Abraham Anghik Ruben. His work is deeply engaged with water, because he takes on contemporary and medieval themes of seafaring, migration, displacement and the environment, and also because he directly and self-consciously addresses continuities of Viking, Norse and Inuit cultures. Ruben sees his mission as that of both artist and storyteller: 'As a storyteller, I have sought to bring life to these ancient voices from a time when these two northern people held a reverence for the land and for all living things therein that provided sustenance and survival.'[24] He has produced thousands of sculptures in a variety of media, including bronze, gold, soapstone, whalebone and narwhal tusks. In this multitude of forms and materials, Ruben's work imagines the untold stories of possible contact between Norse and Inuit peoples, his images evoking mythic and shamanistic common ground often catalysed by water as well as the overarching metaphor of voyage.[25] His interest in the Norse and Inuit relation to their land coincides with his pressing con-cern for the modern environment and issues of climate change, which are similarly major preoccupations of his work. Describing one of many sculptures depicting the sea goddess Sedna, 'Sedna: Life Out of Balance' (see Figures 4.5 and 4.6), for example, he writes:

> This sculpture represents a time of great climatic change which took place in the arctic in the 12th and 13th centuries that led to the decline of Norse settlements and eventually total collapse. This collapse is represented by Sedna, the sea goddess, holding up the world in the form of an iceberg. The few remaining Inuit and Norse people stand and look outwards. This is a mirror to what is happen-ing today.[26]

Ruben's visual storytelling is both a means of remembering and a refusal to forget. His work also chronicles the contemporary migrations and forced displacement of the Inuit, both in the late nineteenth century and in his own experience. In the mid-1950s, the Canadian government removed Inuit children from their families and forced them into residen-tial boarding schools. At age seven Ruben was sent to such a school. In an interview for the *Washington Post* he talks about the experience: 'The best description would be a feeling of being shell-shocked. When they

Figure 4.5 Abraham Anghik Ruben, 'Sedna: Life out of Balance'. Photo courtesy of the Kipling Gallery, Vancouver.

Figure 4.6 Abraham Anghik Ruben, 'Sedna: Life out of Balance' (reverse). Photo courtesy of the Kipling Gallery, Vancouver.

Figure 4.7   Abraham Anghik Ruben, 'Into the Storm: Ragnarok, End of Days'. Photo courtesy of the Kipling Gallery, Vancouver.

brought us in, we were stripped of clothing, showered and changed into new garments and went to roll call. By the time that was done, I had forgotten my parents' names.'[27] The pain of displacement is a theme he returns to frequently and imagines across Norse and Inuit cultures. Given this vital body of work, we were hard-pressed to choose out of thousands of sculptures, but out of the many pieces imaging journeys and boats by Ruben, we settled on this one (Figure 4.7), called 'Into the Storm: Ragnarok, End of Days'.

Here the two-prowed boat faces in two directions, asking the question of where this journey begins or ends – the end of days or the final cataclysm that is Ragnarok in Norse mythology. The boat contains a variety of souls, human and otherwise, at sea, lost or confused, huddling together, seafarers of all stripes on a voyage 'ofer waþuma gebind' ('over the binding of the waves'), as that resonant phrase from *The Wanderer* (line 24) discussed in Chapter 2 has it.

Like Horn's artworks, Ruben's also transform the kinds of conversations we can have with the past. His configurations of the medieval and the modern take the critical practice of the contemporary medieval in another direction, across the Atlantic. His sculptures are passionate, personal, spiritual, political and anchored in history while also redrawing our parameters of space and time. They are simultaneously recognizably and unrecognizably medieval. They imagine momentous cultural passages, and the moments we live now. They too open an epic conversation, figured not as water but as travel on or over the sea: seafaring.

Proposition Six: Seafaring, or being at sea

Seafaring offers another passage – or journey – into our conversation through time and across space. Caroline Bergvall's *Drift* (2014) opens with a looping, slightly baroque re-versioning of the first line of the Old English poem *The Seafarer* ('Mæg ic be me sylfum soð-gied wrecan, / siþas secgan', 'I can tell a true story about myself, speak of my journeys'): 'Let me speak my true journeys own true songs'. These lines open the first 'Song' from *Drift*, a multimedia performance combining voice, sound, music, image and digital film. We described this installation as a 'sonic illumination' when we worked with Bergvall for an event at the Whitechapel Art Gallery in London in 2015, because of how the modern work illuminates and resonates with earlier medieval works.[28] Premiering in 2013 at 'Shorelines: Literature Festival of the Sea' in Southend, Essex, curated by the arts agency Metal, *Drift* asks its audience to think about being at sea, past and present.

The many allusions of Bergvall's first 'Song' about the sea initiate a conversation with its early medieval relation, the Old English poem *The Seafarer*. We particularly like its 'right soggy truth' for Old English 'soð-gied', 'true-telling', or, to pick a later example from the same 'Song', 'caught between whats gone ok whats coming on crossing too close to the cliffs' for Old English 'be clifum cnossað' (*The Seafarer*, line 8). Caught between what's gone, what's coming and what's crossing, to paraphrase this song, are those many passages between past and present explored in *Drift* and *The Seafarer*, but also in Ruben's sculptures of migration and seafaring, as we have seen. After all, the Old English noun 'siþas' in the second line of *The Seafarer*, with its primary meaning of 'journeys', can also be translated as 'experiences'.[29]

Bergvall is increasingly well known to medievalists. Her *Meddle English* of 2011 is a multi-dialectal piece of language poetry excavating, along the way, Chaucerian English, but she is better known as an established, award-winning performance poet, celebrated for her brilliant inventions, to paraphrase Charles Bernstein.[30] *Drift* reworks accounts of early medieval sea travel, such as *The Seafarer* and the journeys of Ohthere and Wulfstan in the Old English version of Orosius's *History*, into a broader repertoire of songs and stories from more recent literary periods. In these ways, the work explores sailing, travelling, drifting, going north and getting lost at sea.[31] *Drift*'s language effects are deliberately estranging and yet strangely familiar. The work moves in and out of modern and historic forms of English, Norwegian and French, crossing the familiar with the unknown, the partially recognized with the historically distant. The first section of *Drift*, entitled 'Seafarer', re-versions the Old English *Seafarer* into sixteen short lyrical 'Songs', drifting between past and present. The sixteen 'Songs' are interspersed with two other groups of poems: 'North', which uses the early medieval narrative of the voyages of Ohthere and Wulfstan as its basis for poetic exploration of what it means to go north, and 'Hafville', loose reworkings from the Icelandic sagas that draw on accounts of seafaring or being 'all at sea', as the Old Icelandic term 'hafvilla' suggests.[32] The second section of *Drift*, 'Report', offers another kind of drifting from the twenty-first century. This time *Drift* opens up a much-expanded perspective on seafaring, and seafarers. It focuses not on those individual, solitary and male travellers on the sea, whose voices and experiences form the basis of 'Seafarer', but on the many modern and diverse travellers at risk because of their seafaring.

'Report' takes up accounts of the so-called 'left-to-die boat' – or, rather, inflated dinghy – of seventy-two refugees forced by the fighting in Tripoli in Libya to attempt the sea crossing to Lampedusa in 2011. This was a journey that presaged the many similarly tragic ones taken across the Mediterranean from North Africa since then. 'Report' intercuts eyewitness statements from survivors of this horrific journey with a verbal and spatio-temporal map showing how a number of authorities (British, American and Italian included) used the complex jurisdiction of the Central Mediterranean to evade their responsibility to rescue those in distress. Bergvall's material for this section was sourced from the Forensic Architecture group at Goldsmiths College, London. Their evidence about the 'left-to-die boat' has been presented to NATO, and used in a number of legal challenges by NGOs; it formed part of a portfolio of work shortlisted for the prestigious award for contemporary art, the Turner Prize, in 2018.[33]

Sixty-three refugees died in the 'left-to-die boat' that drifted for ten days or so in some of the busiest shipping lanes in the world. *Drift* takes up their story to offer a stark reminder of the dangers of being lost at sea and relates it to the poignant hope for a home and to the ethical and aesthetic importance of speaking, finding new forms of bearing witness and telling tales about the sea. At the same time, *Drift* speaks back to the Old English poem, *The Seafarer*, whose final lines exhort the audience, reader or listener to consider where home might be, albeit encouraging an explicitly Christian resolution (lines 117–19) rather than the secular, poetic and political one of *Drift*.

'Report' also talks back to 'Seafarer', the second section of *Drift* is in conversation with the first, and both encourage us to think harder about being at sea, being lost at sea, and, indeed, being all at sea. The first two lines of *The Seafarer*, the true tale ('soð-gied') of the lyric voice or 'I' of the poem, offer us experience as journey ('siþ'), as spoken utterance and as song or poem or 'gied': 'Let me speak my true journeys own true songs'. The lyric voice or 'I' of Bergvall's contemporary, modern 'Song' is similarly rhetorical as well as performative; it expects to be attended to and heard. The parallels with what we know of the performance of and audience for early medieval English poetry – communal, social, oral and aural – are worth noting. So too are the concluding lines of this 'Song': 'Blow wind / blow, anon am I'. The first half of this broken line, 'Blow wind blow', sounds as if it ought to come from *King Lear* or *Moby Dick* or maybe a folk or blues song ('Blow wind blow' by Muddy Waters, perhaps, playing on Waters's name), or the refrain of a Middle English lyric such as 'Blow northerne wynd, blow, blow, blow'.[34] The full line, including its second half, the powerful and alliteratively resonant 'anon am I', is repeated at the end of each of the sixteen 'Songs' in *Drift*. The repetition draws sonic attention to the paradox of the self who speaks (the 'I' of the songs and of the Old English *Seafarer*) and the full force of her chorus-like anonymity: 'anon am I'. Who are or were the selves who speak anonymously, 'anon'? And what are the risks of anonymity in the world, whether historic or modern? 'Blow wind blow, anon am I' invites us simultaneously to consider the repetitive motion of a sea voyage – the self at sea, going somewhere – and the self alone, anon, unidentified and, hence, at sea, out of place, going ... where? We wonder as well about that other meaning of 'anon', an adverb of time, meaning 'at once', 'soon', 'presently', or even 'here'. Being at sea, in this sense, is being here.[35]

Proposition Seven: Getting the drift, or, towards a conclusion

Whether we are at sea, or here, or both, Caroline Bergvall's *Drift* argues that mobility, motion and emotion, are central to our experiences of being in the world, together with its languages, histories, communities and places. The sea, a place of crossing and connecting, is also a cultural resource and a set of ethical practices for remembering peoples, their languages and their histories. Migration is an ethical issue in this poem, as Joshua Davies reminds us.[36] Travel on the sea can be quite literally a matter of life or death, and a reminder of the limits of scholarly and creative interventions in the world. Drifting is risky business. As we have seen, Roni Horn's work also insists on the dangers of watery worlds, which lure the desperate (*Still Water*) and challenge our sense of its resourcefulness

(*The Library of Water*). And the boat in Ruben's *Ragnarok, End of Days* points both ways. Crossing the sea is no easy business.

To catch a wave, to get the drift and to practise drifting are not therefore simply ways to get to the point or to identify a conclusion. Rather, as Proposition One suggests, water is a way of following relationships between the self and the world, bodies and environments, practices and disciplines. So water leads us in Proposition Two to resituate wonder, the practice of wondering, within our knowledge systems, and to examine how wonder has long been a poetic, creative resource. Propositions Three and Four take up the riddling relationship of the self to the world, suggesting how those perpetual relationships, to paraphrase Horn, contour bodies and weather, emotions and worlds. Our pathways into the contemporary medieval take up travel on the sea, seafaring, in Propositions Five and Six. Seafaring in modern and medieval works takes us beyond the metaphorical, or rather to an understanding of how metaphor and literal sense are always mutually implicated; the direction of travel is always going both ways.

So where, then, will the contemporary medieval take us, we wonder? Does our 'epic' conversation hold water? Does it hold out the promise of reorienting our sense of ourselves, our communities, histories

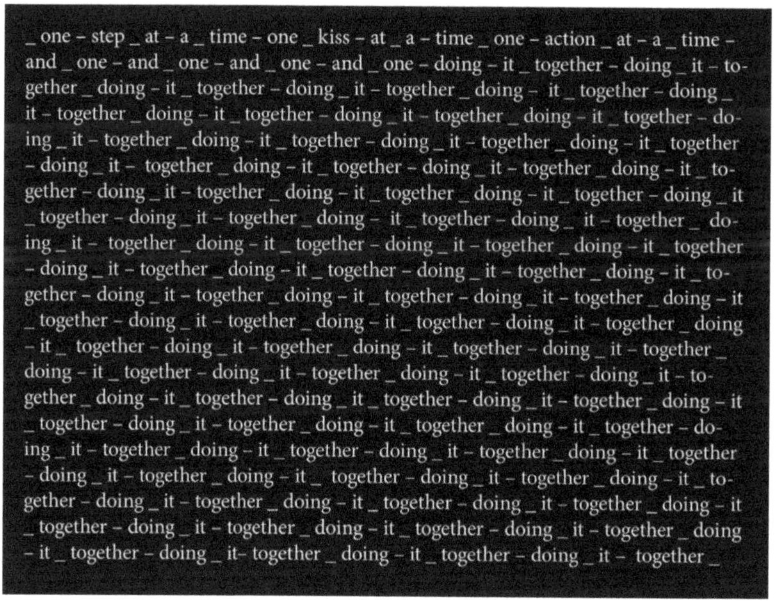

_ one – step _ at – a _ time – one _ kiss – at _ a – time _ one – action _ at – a _ time – and _ one – and _ one – and _ one – and _ one – doing – it _ together – doing _ it – together _ doing _ it – together – doing _ it – together _ doing _ it _ together – doing _ it _ together – doing _ it _ together – doing _ it _ together – doing _ it _ together _ doing – it _ together – doing _ it – together _ doing – it _ together – doing _ it _ together _ doing – it _ together _ doing – it _ together – doing _ it – together _ doing – it _ together – doing _ it _ together _ doing – it _ together _ doing – it _ together _ doing – it _ together – doing _ it – together _ do-ing _ it – together _ doing – it _ together – doing _ it – together _ doing – it _ together – doing _ it – together _ doing – it _ together _ doing – it _ together – doing _ it – together _ doing – it _ together _ doing – it _ together _ doing – it _ together – doing _ it _ together _ doing – it _ together – doing _ it – together _ doing – it _ together – doing _ it – to-gether _ doing – it _ together _ doing – it _ together – doing _ it _ together _ doing – it _ together _ doing – it _ together _ doing – it _ together _ doing – it _ together – do-ing _ it – together _ doing – it _ together _ doing _ it – together _ doing – it _ together _ doing – it _ together _ doing – it _ together – doing _ it _ to-gether – doing _ it – together _ doing – it _ together – doing _ it – together _ doing – it _ together – doing _ it – together _ doing – it _ together – doing _ it – together _ doing _ it _ together – doing _ it – together _ doing – it _ together _ doing – it _ together _ doing – it _ together – do-ing _ it – together _ doing – it _ together _ doing _ it – together _ doing – it _ together _ doing – it _ together _ doing – it _ together – doing _ it _ to-gether – doing _ it – together _ doing – it _ together – doing _ it – together _ doing – it _ together – doing _ it – together _ doing – it _ together _ doing – it _ together _ doing – it _ together _ doing – it _ together – doing _ it – together _

Figure 4.8 Caroline Bergvall, *Together*, 2015, graphic print.
© Caroline Bergvall.

and polities? If working across time enables what we take of and from the past to come into a different focus, then we will be getting somewhere. Together. Concluding this chapter with this image (Figure 4.8) by Bergvall from her Whitechapel Art Gallery residency of 2014 seems apt.

Notes

1. Caroline Bergvall, *Drift* (New York: Nightboat Books, 2014). A good selection of Ruben's work can be seen on his website: http://www.abrahamruben.com/biography/. Accessed 26 January 2019.
2. *Still Water (The River Thames, for Example)*, 1999, fifteen large photolithographs: http://www.tate.org.uk/art/artworks/horn-still-water-the-river-thames-for-example-76675. Accessed 26 January 2019.
3. *Saying Water (The River Thames, for Example)*, by Roni Horn, CD (New York: Dia Center for the Arts, 2001).
4. Roni Horn, *Wonderwater: Alice Offshore*, 4 vols (not numbered), annotated by Louise Bourgeois, Anne Carson, Hélène Cixous and John Waters (Göttingen, Germany: Steidl, 2004).
5. *Wonderwater: Alice Offshore*, annotated by Cixous, 145; *Wonderwater: Alice Offshore*, annotated by Waters, 123.
6. *Ísland: To Place*, 10 vols (Göttingen, Germany: Steidl: 1990–2011); *You Are the Weather* (Zurich: Scalo, 1997); *Weather Reports You* (Göttingen, Germany: Artangel/Steidl, 2007).
7. Clare A. Lees and Gillian R. Overing, 'Women and Water: Icelandic Tales and Anglo-Saxon Moorings', *GeoHumanities* 4.1 (2018), 97–111.
8. All references to the Old English riddles are from George Philip Krapp and Elliott Van Kirk Dobbie, eds, *The Exeter Book* (New York and London: Columbia University Press, 1936). Riddle 69 is on p. 231.
9. Kevin Crossley-Holland, trans., *The Exeter Book Riddles* (Harmondsworth: Penguin Books, 1979), 87.
10. Craig Williamson, ed., *The Old English Riddles of the Exeter Book* (Chapel Hill: University of North Carolina Press, 1977), 106, as Riddle 66.
11. Greg Delanty and Michael Matto, eds, *The Word Exchange: Anglo-Saxon Poems in Translation* (New York and London: W.W. Norton, 2011), 451.
12. For criticism on the Riddles See, for example, Patrick J. Murphy, *Unriddling the Exeter Riddles* (University Park: Pennsylvania State University Press, 2011); Dieter Bitterli, *Say What I am Called: The Old English Riddles of the Exeter Book and the Anglo-Latin Riddle Tradition*, Toronto Anglo-Saxon Series 2 (Toronto: University of Toronto Press, 2009); Mercedes Salvador-Bello, *Isidorean Perceptions of Order: The Exeter Book Riddles and Medieval Latin Enigmata* (Morgantown: West Virginia University Press, 2015); Andy Orchard, 'Enigma Variations: The Anglo-Saxon Riddle-Tradition', in *Latin Learning and English Lore: Studies in Anglo-Saxon Literature for Michael Lapidge*, ed. Katherine O'Brien O'Keeffe and Andy Orchard, 2 vols (Toronto: University of Toronto Press, 2005), vol. 1, 284–304.
13. Peter Ramey, 'Crafting Strangeness: Wonder Terminology in the Exeter Book Riddles and the Anglo-Latin Enigmata', *Review of English Studies* 69.289 (2017): 201–15, at 214–15.
14. Kevin Crossley-Holland gave an overview of the sometimes competing scholarly views of the solutions in *The Exeter Book Riddles*, 103–39. For more recent reviews, see Patrick Murphy, *Unriddling the Exeter Riddles*, and Megan Cavell, ed., *The Riddle Ages: An Anglo-Saxon Riddle Blog*, https://theriddleages.wordpress.com. Accessed 30 January 2019. We follow here Crossley-Holland's suggestions for possible solutions and variants: Riddles 1–3, wind, storm; Riddle 7, swan; Riddle 10, barnacle goose; Riddle 16, anchor; Riddle 22, the circling stars, or the month of December; Riddle 29, moon and sun, or cloud and wind; Riddle 32, ship; Riddle 33, iceberg; Riddle 36, ship; Riddle 41, wisdom, earth, fire, water; Riddle 51, pen and three fingers; Riddle 57, hailstones, raindrops, birds; Riddle 58, well-sweep; Riddle 60, reed-pen; Riddle 66, creation; Riddle(s) 68/69, ice; Riddle 74, cuttlefish, siren, water, swan; Riddle 77, oyster; Riddle 84, water; Riddle 85, fish and river.

15. In his analysis of Riddle 60, *Nonhuman Voices in Anglo-Saxon Literature and Material Culture* (Manchester: Manchester University Press, 2017), James Paz emphasizes the separate materiality of the reed and pen as objects, whereas we envision a dialogue, but he also points to the transformative effect on the self: 'The role of the human in this riddle is to serve as witness to the life and story of a thing, which talks to us, moves among us and organises or reorganises us', 91.

16. Delanty and Matto, eds, *The Word Exchange*, 415.

17. We have translated the Old English noun 'mon' ('man' or 'person') as masculine here, and also in our discussion of *Maxims I* in Chapter 5. Often, the context makes clear a masculine referent; we assume the voices of the protagonists of the poems *The Wanderer* and *The Seafarer*, for example, are male – women do not often go to sea in Old English poetry. There is, however, continuing debate about whether, and when, in the Anglo-Saxon period and thereafter, this is a generic term, inclusive of masculine and feminine. For an overview see Anne Curzan, *Gender Shifts in the History of English* (Cambridge: Cambridge University Press, 2003).

18. 'Uht' ('dawn' or 'the time before daybreak') is the time at which the exiled wanderer must regularly lament his solitary situation; see *The Wanderer*, lines 8–9. All references to *The Wanderer* are from *Old English Shorter Poems*, vol. 2, ed. and trans. Robert E. Bjork, Dumbarton Oaks Medieval Library 32 (Cambridge, Mass., and London: Harvard University Press, 2014), 2.

19. Craig Williamson, trans., *A Feast of Creatures: Anglo-Saxon Riddle-Songs* (Philadelphia: University of Pennsylvania Press, 1982), 120, as Riddle 58.

20. For Hirshfield's version, see Delanty and Matto, eds, *The Word Exchange*, 415.

21. All references to *Beowulf* are to R. D. Fulk, Robert E. Bjork and John D. Niles, eds, *Klaeber's 'Beowulf' and the Fight at Finnsburg*, 4th edn (Toronto: University of Toronto Press, 2008). Translations are our own, unless otherwise indicated.

22. For a comprehensive and ongoing bibliography of 'affect' in multidisciplinary contexts, see Chris Ingraham's website: https://www.cdingraham.com/affect-bibliography. Accessed 18 December 2018.

23. At a critical moment of crossing and passage in the poem. See *The Battle of Maldon*, ed. D. G. Scragg (Manchester: Manchester University Press, 1981), line 89.

24. http://www.abrahamruben.com/biography/. Accessed January 26, 2019.

25. See, for example, 'North Atlantic Saga', described on Ruben's website: 'Using the ivory tusk of the narwhal, Ruben recounts the history of Norse settlement in Iceland and Greenland. The stone base depicts the stylized images of walrus, falcon, and polar bear banded together by an intricate overlay of Norse design elements. Following the natural spiral motion of the tusk, carved figures illustrate men carrying swords; their wives holding agricultural tools; a woman working in the field; a blacksmith at his forge; and figures harvesting the animals of land and sea. The top portion of the tusk envisions a time of contact, trade, and collaborative hunting between Norse settlers and the Thule people, ancestors of Inuit.' http://www.abrahamruben.com/artwork/north-atlantic-saga/. Accessed 26 January 2019.

26. http://www.abrahamruben.com/artwork/sedna-life-out-of-balance/. Accessed 26 January 2019. For a discussion of warming and cooling climate changes in the medieval period see Kenneth Addison, 'Changing Places: The Cistercian Settlement and Rapid Climate Change in Britain', in *A Place to Believe In: Locating Medieval Landscapes*, ed. Clare A. Lees and Gillian R. Overing (University Park: Pennsylvania State University Press, 2006), 211–38. See also Bruce Holsinger, 'Thorkel Farserk Goes for a Swim: Climate Change, the Medieval Optimum, and the Perils of Amateurism', in *The Middle Ages in the Modern World: Twenty-First Century Perspectives*, ed. Bettina Bildhauer and Chris Jones (Oxford: Published for the British Academy by Oxford University Press, 2017), 27–40.

27. DeNeen L. Brown, 'Abraham Anghik Ruben, "the Intermediary": Sculptor Carves Inuit Legends of his Heritage', *Washington Post*, 25 October 2012. http://www.washingtonpost.com/entertainment/museums/abraham-anghik-ruben-the-intermediarysculptor-carves-inuit-legends-of-his-heritage/2012/10/25/6fbbaf12-1d5d-11e2-b647-bb1668e64058_story.html. Accessed 26 January 2019.

28. Bergvall, *Drift*, 2014, 'Song 1', 25.

29. As in Bjork's translation of *The Seafarer* in *Old English Shorter Poems*, 28–9, line 1.

30. Caroline Bergvall, *Meddle English: New and Selected Texts* (New York: Nightboat Books, 2011); for Charles Bernstein's review see https://jacket2.org/commentary/caroline-bergvalls-meddle-english. Accessed 26 January 2019. For recent discussions, see Joshua Davies, *Visions*

and *Ruins: Cultural Memory and the Untimely Middle Ages* (Manchester: Manchester University Press, 2018), 199–206, and David Wallace, *Geoffrey Chaucer: A New Introduction* (Oxford: Oxford University Press, 2017), 138–41.

31. Including such well-known medieval lyrics as 'Sumer is icumen in'. Bergvall's 'Log' in *Drift*, 127–66, offers an account of the processes of composition integral to the work itself.

32. See Bergvall, 'Log', 152–3; see also G. J. Marcus, 'Hafvilla: A Note on Norse Navigation', *Speculum* 30.4 (1955): 601–5.

33. See https://www.forensic-architecture.org/case/left-die-boat/. Accessed 15 September 2018.

34. 'Blow, northerne wynd', *The Harley Lyrics: The Middle English Lyrics of Ms. Harley 2253*, ed. G. L. Brook, 4th revised edn (Manchester: Manchester University Press, 1968), lyric 16.

35. 'anon', adv., *OED Online*. July 2018. Oxford University Press. http://www.oed.com/view/Entry/8053?isAdvanced=false&result=2&rskey=u5kV2N&. Accessed 5 September 2018. The entry traces its etymology to Old English 'an', 'one', 'alone'.

36. Davies, *Visions and Ruins*, 200–1.

5
Environment: self and the world

'Song 16', the final song in 'Seafarer', the first section of Caroline Bergvall's *Drift,* concludes with a variation on the final line of the preceding fifteen songs, amplifying 'Blow wind blow, anon am I' to 'Blow wind blow, anon am I / Everything passes into everything / Anon I pass into everything' (*Drift,* 59). At once, soon, anon, the song suggests, I will pass, blown by the wind, into the world, into everything. Anonymity here is the condition for understanding relations between self and the world. As a resolution to 'Seafarer', these lines defiantly assert the power of anonymous voice – and lyric – in a seafaring world. However, as an introduction to Bergvall's themes of contemporary migration and the 'left-to-die boat' in 'Report', the second section of *Drift,* this final line has a more ambiguous and troubling power. The world and the self are at one, Bergvall's work suggests, and at one and the same time, anonymous or not, we – you and I – share the same fragile and often threatening environment.

Chapter 5 continues our reflection on contemporary medieval practices, but asks what is at stake in the conversation we began in Chapter 4, and for whom? How do we work together, and do things differently, to paraphrase the work by Bergvall with which we concluded that chapter? How are bodies and selves, historic and contemporary, imbricated in environments and worlds? Or, to paraphrase Bergvall, how do bodies pass into worlds? To answer these questions, we draw on ideas of biodegradability. To consider the self as biodegradable is to evoke physicality and biology, pulling us back to bodily process and to the (be)coming together of self as matter and the material environment. We think of this biodegradable self as one which enacts and embodies a symbiosis of self and environment, whence the title of this chapter.

Chapter 5 traces evidence for biodegradable selves in the early medieval culture of Britain and Ireland. It starts, however, by asking how contemporary poets and artists interact with and illuminate biodegradability, and with the broader question of how language with its myriad forms, claims and functions situates the self. We then look at some specific examples of self and environment offered by Old English poetry, before returning briefly to contemporary writing by the chapter's end. Throughout, water offers us an experiential and metaphorical pathway: a means to no end.

Holding water: library, dictionary, self

The Library of Water
(after Roni Horn)

A spinney of glass columns
where books once slept,
saplings of melt water, language illumined.

It sharpens things, altering an element,
as when we made water dance
in a singing bowl

hands beating the meniscus lightly
memory without mark
written on water.

Pauline Stainer[1]

The artist Roni Horn's Library of Water was a library of glacier melt, twenty-four floor-to-ceiling clear glass columns of water that had once been ice … . You could see through the scattered columns, but whatever lay beyond became impossibly broad or thin or halved or twinned or vanished altogether. People became spires and balloons; straight lines bent; islands out the plate-glass windows warped; prismatic edges blurred all boundaries.

Rebecca Solnit[2]

Horn's *Library of Water*, settled on a promontory overlooking Breiðaf-jörður in north-west Iceland, elicits these responses from the British poet Pauline Stainer and the American writer and journalist Rebecca Solnit; both evoke a strong sense of being in place, in the *Library* itself. We too have experienced being in this place and understand that finding any single perspective on this work is itself a challenge. Stainer and Solnit's accounts resonate with, but do not duplicate, the shifting perspectives of our experience as we walked through and among the disappearing glacial waters of Iceland, and saw ourselves fractured and refracted and intersected by the columns of water, and with the landscape and seascape outside the *Library*'s glass walls (Figures 5.1, 5.2 and 5.3). The floor of the *Library*, too, is covered with water, but water in text, water words and phrases, a reminder of the building's past function as a library, a memorial in and to language.[3] As we walk on the floor of water, we are reminded of our physical connection to it. The *Library of Water* contains, grounds and fractures our bodies, its 'prismatic edges' blurring 'all boundaries', as Solnit points out, and it connects this experience – perhaps anchors it – to text, to language, illuminating it, to paraphrase Stainer.

Roni Horn also asks how water and words might be connected in her four-volume artist's book, *Wonderwater*, as we saw in Chapter 4 (Proposition Two). One of the many propositions or prompts that Horn asks of her four very different responders or annotators (Louise Bourgeois, Anne Carson, John Waters and Hélène Cixous), is: 'dictionary of water'. How might such a word compendium of water be imagined or conceptualised? Here are two responses to the phrase, by classicist and poet Anne Carson and artist Louise Bourgeois respectively:

Figure 5.1   Roni Horn, *Water, Selected*, 2003/07. Twenty-four glass columns, each holding approximately 53 gallons/200 litres of water taken from unique glacial sources in Iceland. Permanently installed at Vatnasafn/Library of Water, Stykkishólmur, Iceland. Photo by Stefan Altenburger.

Figure 5.2 Roni Horn, *Water, Selected*, 2003/07. Twenty-four glass columns, each holding approximately 53 gallons/200 litres of water taken from unique glacial sources in Iceland. Permanently installed at Vatnasafn/Library of Water, Stykkishólmur, Iceland. Photo by Roni Horn.

(1)

If you have in you a good mingling of Fire Water Earth Air, you are sound and sensible. If not, not.

(*Wonderwater*, 2, annotated by Anne Carson, 42)

(2)

PRECIOUS LIQUIDS

> Bile
> Blood
> Ear lubricant
> Milk

Figure 5.3   Roni Horn, *Water, Selected*, 2003/07. Twenty-four glass columns, each holding approximately 53 gallons/200 litres of water taken from unique glacial sources in Iceland. Permanently installed at Vatnasafn/Library of Water, Stykkishólmur, Iceland. Photo by Stefan Altenburger.

> Pus
> Saliva
> Semen
> Snot
> Sweat
> Tears
> Urine
>
> (*Wonderwater*, 1, annotated by Louise Bourgeois, 51)

Carson and Bourgeois anchor the concepts of dictionary and of water in the body: Bourgeois's use of bloody red ink is particularly striking. Their responses to Horn's prompt frame a continuum of body and environment, the quotidian and the cosmological, the classical traditions of bodily humours and the un-metaphorized effluents of our always liquid selves. Both offer indices of an always evolving and permeable biodegradable self.[4] What is less commensurate, however, is the relation between the apparent fixity of language evoked by the idea of a dictionary and the fluid media of both self and water prompted by Carson's and Bourgeois's annotations. Horn's provocation to respond to 'dictionary of water' demonstrates how hard it is to define water in terms of an embodied self and vice versa, however much these are implicated in one another. *Wonderwater* prompts our realization that any definition of a biodegradable, watery, liquid self is a work in progress. Like the responses of Stainer and Solnit to the *Library of Water*, the responses of Carson and Bourgeois to *Wonderwater* invite us to consider how language might hold water.

Weather words, water words and words in between

The early medieval continuum that conceptualizes the relation of self to world, physical body to environment, and mind and affect to environment, is, in a holistic sense, that which is written comprehensively across social, psychic and cultural dimensions. Picking up on work begun in Chapter 2 and 4, this section follows various paths of this continuum, looking at weather words, water words and words in between. We bear in mind Horn's assertions – also the titles of two of her works – which we invoked in Chapter 4 (Proposition Five): you are the weather, and weather reports you. These assertions are certainly borne out by the poetic synaesthesia implied by Old English compound adjectives such as 'winter-cearig' ('winter-sad/-caring'), 'ferðloca freorig' ('frozen spirit/heart-locker'), 'morgen-seoc' ('morning-sick') and 'æfen-grom' ('evening-fierce'). Many languages describe mental states in physical terms, or rather in terms that can be understood as coterminous with the physical environment, with its seasons, its weather, its feel and flux. In Modern English, for example, we have a hot temper, a cold nature, a warm heart, a mild manner, a brisk mood or a tepid handshake. Old English poetry, we argue, expands the dimensions and possibilities of such language effects. We find poetic synaesthesia crossing over not only lines of sensory perception but boundaries of the material and the non-material, the human and the non-human. For example, where the poet may describe the sea as singing, a warrior's armour can also sing or fail in battle, just like the warrior; like armour, sea sounds can shine; humans and monsters too might be cross- and co-identifiable, as indicated by the use of the term 'aglæca' to describe Beowulf, the dragon, Grendel and his mother.[5] The range of such semantic continua can address the multivalence of an object or reveal the intersecting contours of masculinity, femininity and monstrosity.

Can we find a trace or contour of the body with water, with the environment, with gender – or with all three – in such poetic language? The idea of the weather map in Chapter 4 (Proposition Five) helps us here. Those swirling lines that the meteorologist waves at on the weather report on the evening news – how do we understand them in relation to how they report us, as Horn might put it? Those lines are isobars and isotherms representing patterns of pressure and temperature respectively. But the static quality of the line is a fiction of sorts, designating as it does changes in temperature and pressure over space and time: the line connects points having the same atmospheric pressure at a given time or on average over a given period. Those wavy lines on the weather map offer a visual example of how a metaphor is not one. An Old English poetic example might be the dictionary definition of 'yð', 'a wave of the sea (lit. or fig.)', as Bosworth and Toller have it.[6] Literal or figurative. We like this normative acknowledgement of co-existing dimensions of meaning in which the literal and the figurative do not preclude each other; it is either / and / or both. So, also, with 'holm', one of the many words for 'sea' in Old English, which can also mean 'wave' in both poetry and prose, literally and figuratively, and is also used as an element of place names.[7]

The meanings of Old English words like 'yð' and 'holm' point to a development of our weather map. Isobars and isotherms become ways of understanding the flux of the relation between self and world in which processes of cross-identification are the curving lines of both dissolution and separation, and where different systems might have zones of coinciding similarity and differentiation. Such a mapping has been put into practice by the British poet Geraldine Monk. Her poetic sequence, *They Who Saw the Deep* (2016), uses the shipping forecasts of the Maritime and Coastguard Agency as prompts for her poetic accounts of the deep cultural and material histories of migration, place, being and culture. The first four lines of the Old English poem *The Wanderer*, re-versioned into Modern English, stand at the head of a sequence that reaches into Christian and pre-Christian accounts of migration and environmental catastrophe to forge long lines of continuity between past and present.[8] In both medieval and modern examples of affective weather mapping, our minds and bodies are presented as in dynamic relation with our cultural and physical worlds. Environment fully engages weather, as the Old English adjective 'winter-cearig' ('winter-sad/-caring') suggests. Indeed, the contoured lines between self and the world, body and history, hold and dissolve, demarcate but do not define. To repeat our conclusion to Proposition Four (Chapter 4), they are always going both ways.

We can read a weather map as literal and figurative, as both metaphor and practice. Storms, rough seas, troubled waters and indeed bad weather of all kinds, however, are often read as primarily metaphorical and/or allegorical in Old English poetry. Heide Estes makes this point in her discussion of sea imagery, noting that 'the sea becomes an instrument of divine intervention in human history', a commonplace image for Christian punishment and reward.[9] Estes argues that in *Andreas*, the Old English poetic account of the life of St Andrew, storms at sea, and bad weather in general, are metaphorical punishments for Andrew's lack of faith, or his inability to recognize Jesus.[10] The idea of water as a metaphorical and metaphysical threat is developed in Della Hooke's analysis of its sacred and mystical contexts in early medieval culture and in the pervasive legislation against pre-Christian veneration of water.[11] Notwithstanding these complex dimensions of Christian control over the Anglo-Saxon cultural imaginary, we argue that water runs its own course, intersecting the literary and historical, and the literal and metaphorical.

Working with physical and cultural geographies, for example, Della Hooke and Maren Clegg Hyer show how rivers create, and re-create, the geographical and political terrains of early medieval England, along with its expanding and contracting wetlands and continuous coastline changes.[12] Rivers, like the lines on a map, mark shifting borders: they are deceptively singular. Exploring the 'mutable boundaries' of land and sea in Anglo-Saxon England, Kelley Wickham-Crowley attends to the shifting and liminal aspects of land- and seascapes, suggesting a cognitive and cultural alliance, even comfort, with borders and liminality:

> The mutability of the 'edge' between land and water, as recorded in Anglo-Saxon texts and archaeology, fits with a way of thinking that considered land/water intersections as a habit of perception or vision, coloring and marking more than the physical environment … creating something of a cognitive map for how vision translates into thought and perception, and how the physical environment can reveal conceptual boundaries.[13]

In another essay, Wickham-Crowley focuses on the East Anglian wetlands and their role in shaping narratives about nations and peoples. She points out that the concept of a frontier did not exist in Old English; the closest parallel is the semantically rich but elusive term 'mearc', with its meanings of 'a bounded area or country, a monument erected to show limits, an omen, indicator or characteristic, a sign, badge or brand on a person, a symbol or character other than a letter, etc.'[14] What jumps out in Wickham-Crowley's list is the idea of the mark or symbol as precursor of and interface with the linguistic sign, and its fluid association with land, people and persons. In this far-reaching argument about the East Anglian wetlands, Wickham-Crowley shows how the fens function as metaphors and have a role in the construction of Anglo-Saxon narratives of nation. But they also function on the more literal and textual levels of the place name – 'fen' or 'moor' – and in the details of their defence. By the end of the Anglo-Saxon period, she concludes:

> the frontier of the fens has become one with the boundaries of England itself as a frontier, a microcosm that stands for the greater whole … The fens were still a boundary space, a frontier negotiating new interactions, but they also, in a real sense, shaped and formed a composite history that resisted Norman political and secular power.[15]

Wickham-Crowley's broad geopolitical argument is complemented by Rebecca Pinner's exploration of medieval causeways and communities in East Anglia.[16] In one particular example from the early eleventh century used by Pinner, the long-dead St Edmund (d. 869) appears to a farmer in a vision and asks for a causeway to be built from his monastery at Bury St Edmunds to Ely. The bones of the even longer-dead St Æthelthryth (d. 679) reside across the fenlands in the minster at Ely, and the eleventh-century account of this vision details the complications of cutting swathes of reeds and building a series of bridges in this difficult terrain of marsh or swamp (Latin 'paludis'). Access is the point here. St Edmund's high-handed order to build the causeway, which only one lone monk is prepared to obey, needs to be understood in terms of the vexed history of contested land ownership, competition over relics, gender dynamics and conflicting political and military allegiances between Bury St Edmunds and Ely.[17] What might a 'causeway' (Latin 'via') connect in terms of community, given the essential ambiguities of the cultural value of the fens or wetlands, whose 'wateriness … is both a means of defence and East Anglia's greatest vulnerability'?[18]

These brief examples about the geography and culture of East Anglian fens, wetlands and causeways suggest that dry land, *terra firma*, is not necessarily so for the inhabitants of early medieval Britain. 'Their word for *island* (OE *ealond/igland*), a compound containing water (*ea*) and land (*lond/land*), must have resounded in their minds with a semantic delay to which present-day users of the word are almost deaf,' suggests Winfried Rudolf.[19] And, while we are perhaps not quite 'deaf' to these resonances of water and island, some adjustment of perspective is demanded of us if we are to become more aware of the liminal semantic and cognitive spaces of both medieval and modern. Are we dealing with marsh or moor, water or earth, land or sea, edge or border, defence or vulnerability, limit or expanse, psychological or political terrain? The fenlands' essential mutability, to paraphrase Wickham-Crowley, is matched by a cultural response, a comfort level, if you will, with ambiguities.

We can take this argument about the ambiguity of terrain further. Dichotomies of inner and outer, or metaphoricity and literality, are attenuated by the intervening presence of other, similar dichotomies in Old English poetry, especially those where water seems to flow through and muddy a variety of other kinds of distinctions. Take, for instance, the lines drawn between animal and human, monster and hero, male and female, monster and female, female and hero, female and animal, *terra firma* and not so firm, hall invader and hall guest in *Beowulf*. Place these apparent oppositions into the complicated underground and underwater medium that is Grendel's and his mother's environment; their lair, mere or cave. What kinds of beings are Grendel and his mother? They inhabit both land and water, and neither is clearly described. Beowulf, too, is apparently quite at home in water, and has strength directly parallel to Grendel's; the 'monster' may be able to eat thirty men, but Beowulf famously has the strength of thirty men in his handgrip.[20] And, as we pointed out earlier, all three – as well as the dragon – share the designation of 'aglæca'. *Beowulf* challenges modern readers to negotiate its linguistic difference, to grapple with such semantic ambiguities delineating bodies and selves in and of the world. Sharply drawing distinctions across lines that are 'fuzzy at best, always subject to question and challenge', as Estes notes, particularly those between 'human' and 'natural', contributes to a mindset that removes human involvement in climate change.[21] This is a familiar enough ecocritical point. Our point, however, is that both the metaphoric and the literal need to be revisited, as does the distance of inner from outer, in any formulation of the self and world. Which is exactly what Old English can help us to do. It can help us to formulate just how a metaphor is not one, not singular in relation to any apparent referent. We return to the weather, then, and to a storm which is equally within and without.

Stormy weather

> All men will be sailors then
> Until the sea shall free them
>
> (Leonard Cohen, 'Suzanne')

> Henġest ðā gȳt
> wælfāgne winter   wunode mid Finne;
> h[ē] unhlitme   eard ġemunde,
> þēah þe ne meahte   on mere drīfan
> hrinġedstefnan,   – holm storme wēol,
> won wið winde,   winter ȳþe belēac
> īsġebinde –   oþ ðæt ōþer cōm
> ġēar in ġeardas,   swā nū ġȳt dêð,
> þā ðe synġāles   sēle bewitiað,
> wuldortorhtan weder.   Ðā wæs winter scacen,
> fæġer foldan bearm.   Fundode wreċċa,
> ġist of ġeardum;   hē tō gyrnwræce
> swīðor þōhte   þonne tō sǣlāde,
> ġif hē tornġemōt   þurhtēon mihte,
>
> (*Beowulf*, lines 1127–40)[22]

Hengest then still / a slaughter-stained winter / dwelled with Finn. / He eagerly remembered his home / although he was not able to drive on the sea / the ring-prowed ship – the sea welled with storm / fought against the wind, winter locked the waves / with an icy bond, until another / spring came to the dwellings – as it now still does / that which always observes the seasons / the gloriously bright weather. Then was winter departed / earth's bosom fair. The exile eager to go / the guest from the homestead; he of revenge / thought more than of a sea journey, / whether he might bring about a hostile meeting.

This extract is from the Finnsburg episode in *Beowulf*, a story told by the 'scop' – the Old English term for a poet – in Heorot at the celebratory feast after the hero's victory over Grendel. It is also one of the best-known examples of the relentless grip of the revenge cycle so endemic to Germanic tribal culture and its heroic poetry. Hengest, a Dane, has survived the death of his lord, Hnæf, who was slain by Finn, a Frisian, the husband of his (Hnæf's) sister Hildeburh. Finn tries to create a peace with honour for the Danish survivors, giving them a hall and distributing treasure to Danes and Frisians equally. It doesn't work. Hengest's dilemma is the classic heroic rock and a hard place. The worst indignity is to follow the slayer of your lord, and the alternative is revenge, and more bloodshed – which is what happens. Hengest kills Finn, and takes Hildeburh, who has lost husband, brother and son in the conflict, back to her homeland. The episode demonstrates the spectacular failure of the power of the marriage bond, which cannot prevail over a revenge-driven and death-centred cultural imperative.

This big picture notwithstanding, Hengest's dilemma is drawn in acutely affective terms, mediated and created by the weather. His is emotional and physical lockdown, a paralysis on all fronts; he can't make a move or make a decision; the ship can't move; the sea and the storm are physical barriers that mirror and create his paralysis. We recall those other 'stormy-minded' ('hreoh-mod') warriors discussed in Proposition Five (Chapter 4), who are laid low, overtaken by a turbulent mixture of storm and 'mod', resulting in paralysis and death. Hengest, however, does make a decision, and one which is in turn inspired by weather. His breaking free of the bonds of winter results not in a sea voyage home as the cycle of the seasons and his own desire as an exile might suppose, but in a return to the similarly cyclical imperative of revenge. Here the line on our weather map, the isobar of metaphor, meets and intersects the 'real' line of the literal boat, the actual storm, the barrier of ice. Hengest's inner life merges with and emerges from his weather-beaten environment.

Another example of how the weather reports us, to come back to Horn's formulation, can be found in the Old English *Maxims I* and *II*.[23] Often classified as 'wisdom literature', these are collections of precepts and gnomic sayings arranged non-narratively, offering general and sometimes not very helpful advice and directives on a wide variety of topics, from gender roles to when to plant, from where dragons belong to how to procure a wife. In juxtaposition to Hengest's dilemma, discussed above, or to that of those other warriors in *Beowulf* discussed in Chapter 2 and 4 who eventually give up the ghost when the chaos of the inner storm destroys both clarity and purpose of mind, *Maxims I* posits this scenario:

> Styran sceal mon strongum mode.   Storm oft holm gebringeþ,
> geofen in grimmum sælum;   onginnað grome fundian
> fealwe on feorran to londe,   hwæþer he fæste stonde.
> Weallas him wiþre healdað,   him biþ wind gemæne.
> Swa biþ sæ smilte,
> þonne hy wind ne weceð;
> swa beoþ þeoda geþwære,   þonne hy geþingad habbað,
> gesittað him on gesundum þingum,   ond þonne mid
> gesiþum healdaþ (lines 50–7)[24]

A man should steer a strong mind. The sea often brings a storm, / the ocean in grim seasons – they begin to rush furiously / the dusky waves from afar to land, however it might stand fast. / The walls hold out against them, they share the wind. / So the sea might be peaceable when the winds don't rouse it up; / so peoples are at peace when they have come together, / they settle in a sound situation and hold with their companions.

This excerpt from *Maxims I* offers a vision of a harmony of the mind, body, land, sea, weather and peaceful social and cultural organization, as well as a complex paralleling and balancing of these elements. The mind is steered like a ship; the waves batter the land and human-created structures ('weallas'), but both withstand, both 'share', the wind. With the wind in check, and the sea at peace, people too are peaceable, and sociability and community become possible. Collective and individual balancing of elements external and internal form a continuum, these lines suggest. Or, to put it another way, the self is in continual translation with the environment; it is at once metaphorized and realized in this fluid relation of mental and physical processes. The mind, like the ship at sea, must be steered; the sea brings waves and storms that batter land and walls; if these hold firm and the sea is not roused by storms, the mind settles and social relations can resume. The self is at sea, stormy or calm; it can be steered through all weather.

Furthermore, control of the self in this passage is a curiously two-way street. As with the protagonists of *The Wanderer* and *The Seafarer*, poems that deal centrally with seafaring, the experience of being at sea can be both involuntary and obsessively desired, a parallel journey for body and soul. Being at sea is far from metaphorical, in that it is an intensely physical and often punishing experience for the body in these poems. At the same time, the soul or the psyche may with equal intensity desire the journey or cede its control, for religious or other reasons. Both impulses are simultaneously possible in this complex synchrony of embodied and psychic journeys. And so, by way of insisting that a metaphor is not one, we return to the idea of a two-way street, and to the complex and dynamic synchrony of self and the elements, the mind and the sea in all weathers in *Maxims I*. And to our quotation from Leonard Cohen's song that prefaces this section: freedom from the voyage, from the necessity of being a perpetual 'sailor', is granted by the sea, and by being at sea.

As we noted earlier in this chapter, the storm and the stormy sea are often construed in terms of Christian and biblical metaphorical trial and endurance, and the sea itself can be a symbol of isolation, a place of primal fear. Many Old English words for water express the power and terror that water elicits, and such fear is likely to be far from simply symbolic. Neither is the delight or joy in the sea, or in seafaring, which is also vividly expressed in Old English poetry.[25] In her reading of this same excerpt from *Maxims I*, Jill Frederick argues that 'the metaphoric quality of this passage deepens the sense that the storm's grim state transcends the physical experience of the water's darkness, which is a metaphor for the challenges of life itself.'[26] We argue instead that to perceive the experience of weather and the physical environment as only metaphorical in this way forges difference and separation between the self and the world. Seeing the world and connecting to it in metaphorical terms can result in a distancing of bodies and psyches from the physical, natural world. It can prevent us from seeing the myriad ways that a metaphor may not be one, excluding the presence, reality, and habitability of liminal spaces. Our reading of this excerpt from *Maxims I* follows the storm across and through environmental and psychic zones; like the isobar on the weather map, we hold these zones in both tension and synchrony.

The biodegradable self that we have been tracing in these early medieval examples is in *and* of the world, its elements *and* its weather. And so in the next section we look at examples of words for water that evoke its psychic and social reach.

Waterways

Old English water language provides a window into an immersive, less bifurcated understanding of the relation of body to water, self and environment. Consider the following brief selection of words and compounds.

Our definitions are adapted from Bosworth and Toller's dictionary and the ongoing Toronto *Dictionary of Old English*; they are illustrative rather than exhaustive.[27] We note here that we are by no means the first students of Old English to make a list of words for water. Ælfric, Abbot of Eynsham, a prolific writer of Old English homilies and sermons and monastic teacher in the late tenth and early eleventh centuries, included a list of Old English water words in a grammar and glossary designed for teaching Latin.[28] His list is a more straightforward catalogue, pointing out different terms for rivers, streams, brooks and burns, for example, although it is in a wordlist otherwise dedicated to trees. Our list seeks rather to evoke some of the many places – literal, affective, psychic – that water traverses and creates in Old English. Our selection of these words follows no pattern – some are included because they are personal favourites – and we add a line or two of context in italics freely adapted from the relevant dictionary where we think it adds to the semantic reach:

wæter	water; a body of water, a stream, lake, sea
wæta	moisture, humours, fluid, water, sap, urine
wæd	a ford, shallow water, water that may be traversed
flod	flowing (in) of the tide; flood tide (as opposed to ebb tide); body of (flowing) water; water(s); referring to a stream of words
ea	river, large body of running water
brim	sea, ocean; waters of the sea
lagu	sea, water
yð	a wave of the sea (lit. or fig.) [*sic*]; any liquid, water;
holm	ocean, sea, water; wave; in poetry: sea, water; land rising from/adjacent to water
geofon	sea, ocean
sæ	sea
ear	sea, ocean, wave
ear-gebland	concourse of waters, tumult of waves
wæterælf-adl	water-elf disease, some form of illness (perhaps chickenpox?)
wæter-broga	terror caused by water, the terror of the deep
yþ-gewinn	wave-strife, the billows
yþ-lad	a way across the waves
wæter-egesa	terror caused by water

Grendles mōdor, / … . wæteregesan wunian sceolde, / cealde strēamas (Grendel's mother … had to inhabit the terrible water, the cold streams). *Beowulf*, lines 1258–60.

wæter-fyrhtness	fear of water,
wæter-fæsten	a place protected by water
wæter-gewæsc	land formed by the washing up of earth
wæter-least	want of water

Ðæt folc wearð geangsumod on mode / for ðære wæterleaste (The [people of Israel] were anxious in mind for the want of water). Ælfric's Homily on *Judith*, lines 150–1.[29]

wæter-seocnesse	water-sickness, dropsy
wæter-wædlness	poverty of water, lack of water
brim-gyst	sailor, literally 'sea-guest'
lagu-cræftig	skilled in matters connected with the sea
mere-werig	weary of journeying on the sea
flod-egsa	'flood-terror', i.e. terror of the waters

Flodegsa becwom / gastas geomre (Flood-dread seized on their sad souls). *Exodus*, lines 447–8.[30]

yþ-worigende	wave-wandering
mere-stræt	sea-street; the road which the sea furnishes
flod-blac	pale through fear of the water (i.e. of drowning?), pale as the water
seolh-ȳða	the waves where the seal swims; still water
wæter-stefne	the voice or sound of water
lagu-fæðm	a watery embrace

Yð sio brune / lagufæðme beleolc (The dark wave played round me with its watery embrace). Riddle 60, lines 6–7.[31]

You are the weather and weather reports you. Horn's assertions resonate with many of these Old English water words, as is borne out by our final example in this list, 'lagu-fæðm', 'an embrace of water'. We may hear the voice of water; we may be its guest; we can be skilled in understanding it and identify it as a source of bodily sickness; we can be terrified or made pale by it, or become one with it, pale in likeness to it.

If we now look again at those lines on our weather map and see ourselves reported by them, reflected, contained and fractured by them as we were by those glass columns in Roni Horn's *Library of Water*, if we conceptualize a self that exists in a constant exchange with environment, and think through or imagine the affective and physical experience of the connected processes of both dissolution and resolution, of a self that is indeed fully biodegradable and deeply commensurate with its eco-sphere, where, then, might this early medieval concept of selfhood find a point of crossing or passage into the modern? How might the biodegrad-able self be acknowledged and translated in the contemporary moment?

Pauline Stainer and Rebecca Solnit, whose work we quoted at the beginning of this chapter, can help us navigate this particular crossing between medieval and contemporary culture. For Stainer, working 'after Roni Horn', the *Library of Water* offers a contemporary opportunity to con-sider further how to write on water. Horn's installation of glass columns is a 'spinney'; individual columns are 'saplings'; we are in a forest of water where 'books once slept'. The metaphorical criss-crossing of art installation and library (meltwater and books) 'sharpens things'; the environment of the Icelandic *Library*, past and present, is brought into poetic focus and language itself is newly illumined. The poem illustrates this effect with another image or a memory of sounding water; 'beating the meniscus lightly'. The word 'meniscus', referring here to the curve of the surface ten-sion of water, is also a term used in optics (a mirror, glass or lens) and of the body (the semi-cartilage between joints). Inner and outer, the self and the world, body and water, are all held 'lightly' in poetic tension in Stainer's poem. These metaphors are not one, to follow the argument of this chap-ter; they offer multiple ways in which water makes its mark.

Solnit's record of her visit to Horn's *Library* also registers the chal-lenge to perception that Horn's columns of glacial water evoke. We can see through the 'scattered columns' but what we see 'beyond' is called into question – widened or thinned, 'halved, or twinned' or, like the gla-ciers themselves, on the point of vanishing altogether. There is discom-fort here too as people 'became spires and balloons', straight lines bend and islands are 'warped'. Boundaries between self and other, objects and beings, islands and worlds, are blurred. Solnit has grasped how Horn's work translates world and self, the one thoroughly implicated in the other, in a contemporary poetic evocation of what we envision in this chapter as exemplifying an early medieval biodegradable self.

Notes

1. Pauline Stainer, *Sleeping under the Juniper Tree* (Hexham, Northumberland: Bloodaxe Books, 2017), 24.
2. Rebecca Solnit, *The Faraway Nearby* (New York: Viking, 2013), 165–6.
3. The floor of the *Library of Water* and the glacial columns are distinct installations, respective-ly titled 'You Are the Weather', and 'Water, Selected'; https://www.artangel.org.uk/project/library-of-water/. Accessed 26 January 2019.

4. One argument brings together these two strands of the cultural/religious and the physiological. Rebecca Reynolds asks why fish consumption increased from the earlier part of the Anglo-Saxon period to the later, assembling an interrelated collage of zooarchaeological, environmental and historical markers in 'Food from the Water: Fishing', in *Water and the Environment in the Anglo-Saxon World*, ed. Maren Clegg Hyer and Della Hooke (Liverpool: Liverpool University Press, 2017), 136–51. The principle of humoral balance and its Greek origins was well understood in ecclesiastical circles: 'Diet was believed to be able to impact the humours. The temperament of men, for example, was thought to be able to be quelled by the consumption of fish' (ibid.: 150). Add the potential influence of the late ninth- and early tenth-century reassertion of the Rule of St Benedict and its interdiction against eating meat on Fridays, and we have an early medieval working formulation of 'you are what you eat', or, that the physical self is imbricated in 'environment' in its broadest sense.

5. The term 'aglæca' has been much discussed by Anglo-Saxonists; often translated as 'monster', it is more accurately understood as something like 'awesome or formidable one'. For a variety of viewpoints on the derivation of this term and its translation history, See, for example, Christine Alfano, 'The Issue of Feminine Monstrosity: A Reevaluation of Grendel's Mother', *Comitatus* 23.1 (1992): 1–16, and Signe M. Carlson, 'The Monsters of *Beowulf*: Creations of Literary Scholars', *Journal of American Folklore* 80.318 (1967): 357–64.

6. *An Anglo-Saxon Dictionary*, J. Bosworth and T. Northcote Toller (Oxford: Clarendon Press, 1898); *An Anglo-Saxon Dictionary: Supplement*, T. Northcote Toller (Oxford: Clarendon Press, 1921); http://bosworth.ff.cuni.cz. Accessed 30 January 2019.

7. 'holm', n. *The Dictionary of Old English A to I*. University of Toronto: https://tapor.library.utoronto.ca/doe/. Accessed 30 January 2019.

8. Geraldine Monk, *They Who Saw the Deep* (Anderson, S.C.: Parlor Press, 2016), 5–27, with epigraph, 5. Old English traditions of prediction on the basis of observed natural phenomena, prognostics, are particularly relevant here. For examples see *Anglo-Saxon Prognostics: An Edition and Translation of Texts from London, British Library, MS Cotton Tiberius A.iii*, ed. Roy M. Liuzza (Cambridge: D. S. Brewer, 2011); see also Marilina Cesario, 'Weather Prognostics in Anglo-Saxon England', *English Studies* 93.4 (2012): 391–426.

9. Heide Estes, *Anglo-Saxon Literary Landscapes: Ecotheory and the Environmental Imagination* (Amsterdam: Amsterdam University Press, 2017), 42.

10. Estes, 38–40.

11. Della Hooke, 'Rivers, Wells and Springs in Anglo-Saxon England: Water in Sacred and Mystical Contexts', in *Water and the Environment in the Anglo-Saxon World*, ed. Maren Clegg Hyer and Della Hooke (Liverpool: Liverpool University Press, 2017), 107–35, at 120–1.

12. 'Introduction', in *Water and the Environment in the Anglo-Saxon World*, ed. Clegg Hyer and Hooke, 1–14, at 1–10. See also Bethany Whalley's PhD thesis, 'Currents of History: Water and Waterways in Early Medieval Culture and the Contemporary Arts'. King's College London, 2019.

13. Kelley M. Wickham-Crowley, 'Living on the *Ecg*: The Mutable Boundaries of Land and Water in Anglo-Saxon Contexts', in *A Place to Believe In: Locating Medieval Landscapes*, ed. Clare A. Lees and Gillian R. Overing (University Park: Pennsylvania State University Press, 2006), 85–110, at 85.

14. Kelley M. Wickham-Crowley, 'Fens and Frontiers', in *Water and the Environment in the Anglo-Saxon World*, ed. Clegg Hyer and Hooke, 68–88, at 83. See also Bosworth and Toller, s.v. 'mearc'.

15. 'Fens and Frontiers', 88. See also Susan Oosthuizen, 'Culture and Identity in the Early Medieval Fenland Landscape', *Landscape History*, 37.1 (2016): 5–24, and more generally *The Anglo-Saxon Fenland* (Oxford: Windgather Press, 2017). For a reading which considers the liminality of these spaces in both political and religious contexts, see Catherine A. M. Clarke, 'Edges and Otherworlds: Imagining Tidal Spaces in Early Medieval Britain', in *The Sea and Englishness in the Middle Ages: Maritime Narratives, Identity and Culture*, ed. Sebastian I. Sobecki (Cambridge: D. S. Brewer, 2011), 81–101.

16. Rebecca Pinner, 'Thinking Wetly: Causeways and Communities in East Anglian Hagiography', *Open Library of Humanities* 4.2 (2018): 2–49. DOI: http://doi.org/10.16995/olh.229.

17. See Pinner, 'Thinking Wetly', 22–8.

18. Pinner, 'Thinking Wetly', 9.

19. Winfried Rudolf, 'The Spiritual Islescape of the Anglo-Saxons', in *The Sea and Englishness in the Middle Ages*, ed. Sobecki, 31–57, at 31.

20. For a detailed discussion of these various ambiguities, see Gillian R. Overing, 'Beowulf on Gender', New Medieval Literatures 12 (2010): 1–22.
21. Heide Estes, Anglo-Saxon Literary Landscapes, 58. On revising distinctions between the human and the natural, see also James Paz, Nonhuman Voices in Anglo-Saxon Literature and Material Culture (Manchester: Manchester University Press, 2017).
22. All references to Beowulf are from R. D. Fulk, Robert E. Bjork and John D. Niles, eds, Klaeber's 'Beowulf' and the Fight at Finnsburg, 4th edn (Toronto: University of Toronto Press, 2008). Translations are our own, unless otherwise indicated.
23. For Maxims I, see George Philip Krapp and Elliott Van Kirk Dobbie, eds, The Exeter Book, Anglo-Saxon Poetic Records 3 (New York: Columbia University Press, 1936), 156–63. For Maxims II, see Elliott Van Kirk Dobbie, ed., The Anglo-Saxon Minor Poems, Anglo-Saxon Poetic Records 6 (New York: Columbia University Press, 1942), 55–7. For an overview, see Paul Cavill, Maxims in Old English Poetry (Cambridge: D. S. Brewer, 1999).
24. Maxims I, 158.
25. See Estes, Anglo-Saxon Literary Landscapes for a discussion of the complexity and variety of representations of the sea in both secular and religious poetry, 35–59. See also Paz, Nonhuman Voices.
26. Jill A. Frederick, 'From Whale's Road to Water under the Earth: Water in Anglo-Saxon Poetry', in Water and the Environment in the Anglo-Saxon World, ed. Hyer and Hooke, 15–32, at 22.
27. Dictionary of Old English: A to I online, ed. Angus Cameron, Ashley Crandell Amos, Antonette diPaolo Healey et al. (Dictionary of Old English Project, University of Toronto Centre for Medieval Studies, 2018): https://tapor.library.utoronto.ca/doe/. Accessed 11 April 2019. An Anglo-Saxon Dictionary, J. Bosworth and T. Northcote Toller (Oxford: Clarendon Press, 1898); An Anglo-Saxon Dictionary, Based on the Manuscript Collections of the Late Joseph Bosworth: Supplement, T. Northcote Toller (Oxford: Clarendon Press, 1921); http://bosworth.ff.cuni.cz. Accessed 30 January 2019.
28. Ælfrics Grammatik und Glossar, ed. Julius Zupitza (Berlin: Weidmann, 1880), 313. With thanks to Lily Armstrong, and for further discussion see her '"Inscientibus pueralis, non senibus": Ælfric's Grammar out of Context in Oxford MS Barlow 35' (MSt dissertation, University of Oxford, 2018).
29. As Bosworth and Toller, An Anglo-Saxon Dictionary. Contrast the more recent version of this homily in S. D. Lee, ed., Ælfric's Homilies on 'Judith', 'Esther', and the 'Maccabees' (1999): http://users.ox.ac.uk/~stuart/kings/. Accessed 31 May 2019.
30. George Philip Krapp, ed., The Junius Manuscript, Anglo-Saxon Poetic Records 1 (New York, Columbia University Press, 1931), 90–107.
31. George Philip Krapp and Elliott Van Kirk Dobbie, eds, The Exeter Book, Anglo-Saxon Poetic Records 3 (New York and London: Columbia University Press, 1936), 225.

6
In translation

Translation, as both practice and concept, has emerged during the course of this book as one of its key themes. Translation is a form of communication, and it is one way past cultures enter the contemporary. Translating from an old language into a modern one is perhaps the most familiar practice for medievalists, especially those whose work is based in textual culture. Translation is a scholarly skill, then, but it is also a poetic practice, and this book has drawn on the work of contemporary poets such as Caroline Bergvall, Sharon Morris and Pauline Stainer as ways to explore the contemporary medieval. Translation is also transformation. It is a practice that expresses dynamic, transformative relationships between languages and times, as Chapter 4 argued, and between self and the world, as Chapter 5 explored. The ethical and the aesthetic as well as the social and the cultural are all implicated in translation. This concluding chapter focuses on the dynamism that translation as both practice and concept expresses. Translation is a means of travel, of transit. In this final chapter, we test what it might mean to be 'in' translation. We turn to contemporary art-making, in contrast with the focus on earlier medieval culture in Chapter 5, to explore some further implications of the contemporary medieval.

This book has considered contexts large and speculative (contemporary art-making and the creative-critical environment), and small and quotidian (the weather, words for water). We offer these as contributions to an ongoing conversation about the contemporary medieval in practice. In Chapter 5 we looked to the early medieval for our study of the environment and the ethics of understanding bodies, identities and histories. In Chapter 4, we found a thread through time that explored not only wonder but also travail and duress, loneliness, exile and displacement, the psyche in extremis. We focused attention on questions of audience, both early medieval and modern, in Chapter 3, and took a long look at our own scholarship, linked and laced through time, in Chapter 2. Throughout, we have found ourselves in conversation with present and past. Our reflections have offered us practices for understanding the contemporary medieval. We experience these passages between past and present as forms of translation that, in turn, translate us; they enable us to be in transit, and to remain open to the generative possibilities of both the contemporary and the medieval.

We offer these concluding remarks as a meditation on the further questions that our study of the contemporary medieval has raised and might address. Given our emphasis on seafaring and travel in Chapter 4, how might present realities of displacement, migration and exile be illuminated by their intersection with the medieval? How might our interest in the medieval biodegradable self in Chapter 5 intersect with the current threat of climate change – an issue we first raised in Chapter 2? What further light might the contemporary medieval shed on our current psychic and political engagement with the environment? How will the thread of water that we have followed throughout this book reveal the felt dimensions of racial injustice? Following Bergvall's *Drift*, how might an anonymous seafarer or wanderer, like those of the Old English poems that are now named for them, speak to the migrant or the refugee of the present moment? What might be the healing, inspiring, creative outcomes and possibilities for our many selves, our forms of communication and writing, our scholarship, our pedagogies of our ongoing conversation about the contemporary medieval?

The dynamic relation between selves and worlds in transit, both medieval and modern, opens up the fluidity of identity in physical and psychic ways. We have explored how contemporary art-making offers passages to, and from, the medieval by using the work of Roni Horn as well as of Caroline Bergvall. Carol Ann Duffy's *Everyman* also tackles worlds and selves, taking on religion in its broadest cultural and social contexts. Abraham Anghik Ruben's work speaks to our current refugee crises by addressing the particular environments, cultures and histories of the Inuit. Artists like Horn (whose work is central to Chapter 4), Katie Paterson and Olafur Eliasson (both of whom we discussed briefly in Chapter 2) speak to the questions and concerns about deep time and the environment we bring to the table as medievalists, but they do not engage directly with the medieval past. So too, in this chapter, artists such as Philip Ob Rey, Edward Burtynsky and M. NourbeSe Philip help us resist an ending. Exploring the work of these contemporary artists and poets advances and expands the dimensions of the contemporary medieval. This work creates different continua and a new set of contours in and into which the contemporary self is translatable, expanding the reach of our weather-mapping of self and environment (addressed first in Chapter 2 and more fully in Chapter 4). Like Horn, Bergvall and Ruben, Ob Rey, Burtynsky and Philip bring pressing modern political, environmental and ethical issues to the forefront of our conversation with the early medieval past.

In an apposite, and opposing, vision of contemporary biodegradability, the '"V" HS' series for *Humantropy* (2015) by the French, Iceland-based video and multimedia artist Philip Ob Rey offers a photographic installation of giant forms made from discarded and tangled webs of VHS tapes, located in particularly bleak Icelandic landscapes. These giant figures or creatures, formed from the detritus of old media, make a powerful protest against both plastic pollution and contemporary mass media. They also conjure the stuff of a variety of nightmares, both medieval and contemporary. As a commentary on the evolution and devolution of Norse giants and monsters, these giants evoke the Icelandic medieval past as well as a desolate modernity and futurity.[1] These installations also evoke a contemporary nightmare in which the absence of biodegradability becomes a material threat to ourselves. This vision of a psyche severed from the environment and haunted by monstrous forms of its own making offers a stark contrast to the relative fluidity and potential harmony of the early medieval biodegradable self we have proposed. However, Ob Rey's work also helps us insist that we offer no idealization of any concept of medieval biodegradability. The detritus of the early medieval world and its rubbish dumps are well documented by modern archaeology, and the examples of degradability we discuss in Chapter 5 are shot through with issues of power (the building of bridges across the fens, for examples) as well as terror (water is a source of distance as much as it is of desire, as our example from *Maxims I* demonstrates). Ob Rey's Norse-inspired giants express the scale of the contemporary problem.

Another modern artist, whose work is entirely non-medieval, addresses similar questions of scale that also recall Horn's art-practice, and pull us back to our pervasive themes of water and the environment. Edward Burtynsky's monumental compendium of aerial photographs, *Burtynsky: Water*, often realizes water in terms of its profound absence, and the insistent presence of that absence in the landscape.[2] The images shift perspective entirely, upending our visual and affective assumptions.[3] His photographs of the Colorado River Delta in Baja, Mexico, for example, look like massive sprawling tree shapes at first sight, spanning out to branches, twigs and leaves in remarkable detail.[4] The trunk of this delta only has a sliver of blue or green. The browns and greys of the rest of the 'tree' detail the absence of water. The delta becoming desert. The tree that is becoming petrified, a petroglyph. The tree that was a river. The uncanny beauty and haunting disjunctions of these images of absence are a memorial to water and a refusal to forget the harsh realities of climate change. Aesthetics is a way to negotiate ethics.

'Water is the reason we can say its name' is the opening dedication, or epitaph, to Burtynsky's collection. The statement offers us the chance to reflect once more on the importance of naming and speaking water, as well as the connection of the very existence of water to our speaking its disappearance. We recall here Roni Horn's *Library of Water*, which we explored first in Chapter 2 and to which we returned in Chapter 4 and 5. Rebecca Solnit's assessment of its testimony to transience, '[t]he pillars of water from all over Iceland made the room Iceland in miniature and a memorial for what was not yet gone', complement Pauline Stainer's vision of the *Library* as 'memory without mark / written on water'.[5] In *Wonderwater*, Roni Horn offered the phrase 'dictionary of water' as a prompt for her interlocutors, Louise Bourgeois, Hélène Cixous, Anne Carson and John Waters, thereby posing the question of how water is collected, stored and remembered. Prompted in turn by Solnit, Stainer and Horn, we pose the related question, 'How do you remember the future?' The *Library of Water* is a profound link to a disappeared past and a disappearing future. At the same time, it offers a way to formulate an environmental consciousness that moves beyond nostalgia and regret to forge deep cultural and psychic connections to water.

The passage of water, the connectivity it forms with historical selves, and the importance of remembering that which cannot be expressed (How do you say water?, as Horn puts it) is differently realized in the poetry of Canadian and Caribbean writer, M. NourbeSe Philip. NourbeSe Philip is another contemporary artist who does not directly engage with the medieval. Her epic poem *Zong!* evokes the terror of exile, abandonment and shipwreck, and the complete watery dissolution and effacement of enslaved African bodies.[6] The poem offers a poetic re-versioning of the partial – both fragmentary and biased – historical documents that record the fate of the slave ship *Zong*. In November 1781, the captain of this ship, Collingwood, ordered its cargo of 150 slaves to be cast overboard and left to drown, an act that enabled the ship's owners to claim money from insurance. NourbeSe Philip's work is based on the only extant public document related to this massacre; it reworks its sparse and formulaic legal language into English-language poetry while remembering the multiple languages that might have been spoken on that ship. NourbeSe Philip describes her intention to use the legal language of the case brought to court as a 'word store' by which she was able to lock herself into the work of poetry, a form of limitation that creates a space in which to recall the unspoken, the silent words of the slaves locked in the ship's hold.[7] Such arrangement and rearrangement based on a finite source might remind us of the Old English poet's use of a 'wordhoard', a set of oral-formulaic building blocks, by means of which the text or performance will be reinvented, or redesigned, with each telling. But NourbeSe Philip takes this principle and wrenches it into another dimension of both reading and listening:

> I murder the text, literally cut it into pieces, castrating verbs, suffocating adjectives, murdering nouns, throwing articles, prepositions, conjunctions overboard, jettisoning adverbs: I separate subject from verb, verb from object – create semantic mayhem … and like some seer, sangoma, or prophet who, having sacrificed an animal for signs and portents of a new life, or simply life, reads the untold story that tells itself by not telling.[8]

Words here are murdered, in poetic acts that recall the murder of all those slaves. We are also drawn to this poem not only because it expands the parameters and possibilities of our medieval modes of 'interlace' and association, but because it recalls similar themes and engages a similar practice of 'forensic listening' to that demanded by Bergvall's *Drift* (discussed in Chapter 4).[9] The question of what it means to be 'at sea' drifts uncannily across the centuries when we consider the Old English exile, those enslaved on the eighteenth-century ship *Zong*, or those trapped on the twenty-first-century 'left-to-die boat'. Both Bergvall and NourbeSe Philip invite us to reflect further on anonymity, past and present, and to find spaces where silence in the historical record might occasion a practice of remembrance. For Bergvall, songs offer ways to speak the dispersed and distributed anonymous self, as we have seen. NourbeSe Philip notes how close are 'song' and 'Zong', itself an overwriting of the original Dutch name of the ship, '*Zorg*'. In *Drift* and in *Zong!* the past finds its voice by participating in broken song, in the wrenched and displaced poetry of the present. *Zong!* goes further to acknowledge ancestral co-authorship: the poem is credited to the poet 'as told by Setaey Adamu Boateng'; the work is presented as a collaboration between past and present.

Analogous to NourbeSe Philip's decentring of Western conventions of authorship is the immersive installation of *Typhoon Coming On* (2018) by black American artist Sondra Perry.[10] The work digitally manipulates J. M. W. Turner's painting *Slave Ship*, first exhibited in 1840 as *Slavers Throwing Overboard the Dead and Dying – Typhoon Coming On*, which was itself inspired by accounts of the *Zong*. Perry's ocean is created digitally, using open-source software for visual and sonic immersion. In *Typhoon Coming On*, new technologies are the means for the entanglement of identity and experience: black histories shape and undo work made about them by British artists in the past. In this most recent iteration of the story of the *Zong*, as in *Zong!* and *Drift*, water remains the consistent catalyst and medium for these themes of exile, displacement and annihilation. Water remains central to understanding our passages to and from the medieval.[11]

Like Abraham Anghik Ruben's sculptures that tell a cultural story of two Northern peoples, the medieval Norse and the indigenous Inuvialuit, Caroline Bergvall's *Drift* and M. NourbeSe Philip's *Zong!* span centuries and take on terror, strangeness and compelling human journeys. They do indeed speak the past, and to the past, in epic terms. But there are more quotidian places to pursue this epic conversation, with our students and with each other, and therefore we include here a brief anecdote from one of Gillian's experiences of undergraduate teaching at Wake Forest University, North Carolina. The scene is an interdisciplinary first-year seminar, called 'Making Light of the Dark Ages', where few students got the intended pun, primarily because half of them were non-native speakers, from China, Indonesia and Sri Lanka. This had been an unusually reserved group, perhaps because of the language barrier, perhaps because of cultural conventions which did not encourage speaking out in class, and also because the material can be both alien and challenging, even disconcerting. The course texts were a mix of medieval and modern, literary and historical, and ranged from R. I. Moore's work on persecution in the early medieval period to the obligatory *Monty Python and the Holy Grail* showings, all in the service of making light of the so-called 'Dark Ages', having some creative-critical fun with the modern understandings of the medieval and learning some history at the same time.[12]

Four students chose to do a final team presentation on *The Wanderer*, focusing on different passages from the poem and on the general theme of emotion. They asked, What does it feel like to be lonely, homesick, on a journey, yearning, adrift? What could they learn from this most sober of Old English poems about feeling, about being in the world, in this present world? Each student had glossed passages from *The Wanderer* that they identified with a particular emotional state such as isolation, depression, confusion, regret or nostalgia. Certainly, they detected no joy in this experience of being 'at sea'. They had carefully looked at the nuances of different translations of the Old English, and then recalled a contemporary song lyric and an experience in their own lives in which they identified with the wanderer. These four of the most reserved students in the class described with incisive clarity their own instances of pain and loss, their own experiences of being in exile in the USA and in some cases in their homelands, understanding them through the lens of this poem which they claimed enabled them to give voice to their own experience. While this proved to be a moving and meaningful teaching experience and indeed far from depressing, it was also one which raised the question of just what was being taught. Does the medieval poem disappear as the students make it their own? Or does it come into its own? What kind of transaction is taking place? Do the students translate the poem, or are they translated by it? We would argue both, and that these students contribute to and participate in the epic conversation developed by many of the artists we have discussed. They found one expression of the language in which they could conduct that conversation, and, as Clare's account of the poetry bus in Chapter 1 also demonstrated, it is finding a language to express the contemporary medieval that is key.

Teaching the contemporary medieval is one further way to develop a conversation with the past that challenges and enriches our present. It is another place where we can continue to explore how we might speak the early medieval world, and to explore the problem and challenge of audience to identify how we can include non-medievalists of all stripes, and indeed the many types of medievalists, in this conversation. The stakes, we believe, are high in that the profound human dilemmas we now experience, whether these be political, racial or environmental, are brought into sharp relief and are given a new affective and potentially activist dimension. We of course would argue as humanist scholars that any study of the humanities will make us more fully human, but we have found, in our own experience of both studying and working with many different artists, new forms of creative engagement, and an explosive new frontier of artistic energy and innovation that is inspired by the early medieval world. The energy and beauty of the contemporary medieval has inspired us in turn, and this is what we want to pass on; this is a conversation we would like to continue.

Notes

1. http://www.humantropy.com/. Accessed 26 January 2019. See also https://www.instagram.com/p/BE5kk5OwoC2/?taken-by=humantropy. Accessed 26 January 2019.
2. Edward Burtynsky, *Burtynsky: Water* (Göttingen, Germany: Steidl, 2013).
3. Some of these images are currently available online: https://www.edwardburtynsky.com/projects/photographs/water/. Accessed 18 December 2018.

4. *Burtynsky: Water*, Plates 34, 35.
5. Rebecca Solnit, *The Faraway Nearby*, 166; Pauline Stainer, 'The Library of Water', *Sleeping under the Juniper Tree*, 24.
6. M. NourbeSe Philip, *Zong!* (Middletown, Conn.: Wesleyan University Press, 2008).
7. *Zong!*, 191.
8. *Zong!*, 193–4. See, for example, 32 and 34 for ways in which the poem represents visual and semantic 'breakdown' of water graphically.
9. We are not the first to link these two poems. See, for example, Adalaide Morris, 'Forensic Listening: NourbeSe Philip's "Zong!", Caroline Bergvall's "Drift", and the Contemporary Long Poem', *Dibur Literary Journal* 4 (Spring 2017): 77–87.
10. *Typhoon Coming On*, by Sondra Perry, was shown at the Serpentine Gallery, London in 2018: https://www.serpentinegalleries.org/exhibitions-events/sondra-perry-typhoon-coming-on. Accessed 26 January 2019.
11. Other important artworks addressing migration include Isaac Julien's multi-screen *Western Union: Small Boats* (2007): https://www.isaacjulien.com/projects/western-union-small-boats/ and John Akomfrah's three-screen installation for the 2015 Venice Biennale, *Vertigo Sea*: https://www.turnercontemporary.org/exhibitions/john-akomfrah-vertigo-sea. Both accessed 26 January 2019.
12. R. I. Moore, *The Formation of a Persecuting Society: Power and Deviance in Western Europe, 950–1250* (Oxford: Basil Blackwell, 1987), and *Monty Python and the Holy Grail*, dir. Terry Gilliam and Terry Jones, 1975.

Bibliography

Works, editions and translations

Ader, Bas Jan. *Fall 1, Los Angeles*. 1970.

Ader, Bas Jan. *Broken Fall (Organic)*. 1971.

Ælfric. *Ælfrics Grammatik und Glossar*. Edited by Julius Zupitza. Berlin: Weidmann, 1880.

Ælfric. *Ælfric's De Temporibus Anni*. Edited and translated by Martin Blake. Cambridge: D. S. Brewer, 2009.

Akomfrah, John. *Vertigo Sea*, premiered at the Venice Biennale. 2015. Last modified 26 January 2019. https://www.turnercontemporary.org/exhibitions/john-akomfrah-vertigo-sea.

Anlezark, Daniel. Ed. and trans. *Genesis*. In *Old Testament Narratives*, Dumbarton Oaks Medieval Library 7. Cambridge, Mass.: Harvard University Press, 2011, 1–203.

Battle of Maldon, The. Edited by D. G. Scragg. Manchester: Manchester University Press, 1981.

Bede. *Ecclesiastical History of the English People*. Edited by B. Colgrave and R. A. B. Mynors. Oxford: Clarendon Press, 1969; rev. edn Oxford University Press, 1991.

Bede. *Bede: 'On the Nature of Things' and 'On Time'*. Translated by Calvin B. Kendall and Faith Wallis. Liverpool: Liverpool University Press, 2010.

Bede. *Bede: 'The Reckoning of Time'*. Translated by Faith Wallis. Liverpool: Liverpool University Press, 1999.

Bergvall, Caroline. *Meddle English: New and Selected Texts*. New York: Nightboat Books, 2011.

Bergvall, Caroline. *Drift*. New York: Nightboat Books, 2014.

Bjork, Robert E. Ed. and trans. *Old English Shorter Poems. Volume II: Wisdom and Lyric*. Dumbarton Oaks Medieval Library 32. Cambridge, Mass., and London: Harvard University Press, 2014.

Brook, G. L. Ed. *The Harley Lyrics: The Middle English Lyrics of Ms. Harley 2253*. 4th rev. edn. Manchester: Manchester University Press, 1968.

Bruegel, Pieter, the Elder. *Landscape with the Fall of Icarus*. c. 1555. Last modified 20 January 2019. https://www.bl.uk/collection-items/landscape-with-the-fall-of-icarus.

Bryce, Colette. Ed. *Shadow Script: Twelve Poems for Lindisfarne and Bamburgh*. Newcastle University: Newcastle Centre for the Literary Arts, 2013.

Burtynsky, Edward. *Burtynsky: Water*. Edited by Marcus Schubert. With essays by Wade Davis and Russell Lord. Göttingen: Steidl, 2013.

Burtynsky, Edward. https://www.edwardburtynsky.com/projects/photographs/water/. Last modified 18 December 2018.

Cawley, A. C. Ed. *Everyman and Medieval Miracle Plays*. London: J. M. Dent, 1956; new edn 1993.

Crossley-Holland, Kevin. Trans. *The Exeter Book Riddles*. Harmondsworth: Penguin Books, 1979.

Davidson, Clifford, Martin W. Walsh and Ton J. Broos. Eds. *Everyman and Its Dutch Original, Elckerlijc*. Kalamazoo, Mich.: Medieval Institute Publications, 2007.

Dean, Tacita. *And He Fell into the Sea*, 1996.

Delanty, Greg and Michael Matto. Eds. *The Word Exchange: Anglo-Saxon Poems in Translation*. New York and London: W. W. Norton, 2011.

Drew, Richard. *The Falling Man, September 11, 2001*. 2001.

Duffy, Carol Ann. *Standing Female Nude*. London: Anvil Press Poetry, 1985; repr. London: Picador, 2016.

Duffy, Carol Ann. *Everyman: A New Adaptation*. London: Faber & Faber, 2015.

Duffy, Carol Ann. *Everyman*. National Theatre. Directed by Rufus Norris. 2015. Last modified 30 July 2018. https://www.youtube.com/watch?v=la0Zg_0Vc9s (trailer).

Ejiofor, Chiwetel. Interview on *Everyman*. Last modified 2 February 2019. http://ntlive.nation-altheatre.org.uk/productions/50433-everyman.

Eliasson, Olafur and Minik Rosing. *Ice Watch*. Last modified 29 December 2018. https://www.tate.org.uk/whats-on/tate-modern/exhibition/olafur-eliasson-and-minik-rosing-ice-watch.

Exeter Book, The. Ed. George Philip Krapp and Elliott Van Kirk Dobbie. Anglo-Saxon Poetic Records 3. New York and London: Columbia University Press, 1936.

Finer, Jem. *Longplayer*. Last modified 25 June 2018. http://longplayer.org/about/.

Forensic Architecture. 'The Left-to-Die Boat.' Last modified 15 September 2018. https://www.forensic-architecture.org/case/left-die-boat/.

Fulk, R. D., Robert E. Bjork and John D. Niles. Eds. *Klaeber's 'Beowulf' and the Fight at Finnsburg*. 4th edn. Toronto: University of Toronto Press, 2008.

Gilliam, Terry and Terry Jones. Dirs. *Monty Python and the Holy Grail*, 1975.

Horn, Roni. *Ísland: To Place*. 10 vols. Göttingen, Germany: Steidl, 1990–2011.

Horn, Roni. *You Are the Weather*. Zurich: Scalo, 1997.

Horn, Roni. *Still Water (The River Thames, for Example)*. Fifteen large photolithographs. 1999. Last modified 30 June 2018. http://www.tate.org.uk/art/artworks/horn-still-water-the-river-thames-for-example-76675.

Horn, Roni. *Saying Water (The River Thames, for Example)*. CD. Dia Center for the Arts, New York, 2001.

Horn, Roni. *Wonderwater: Alice Offshore*, 4 vols (not numbered), annotated by Louise Bourgeois, Anne Carson, Hélène Cixous and John Waters. Göttingen, Germany: Steidl, 2004.

Horn, Roni. *Vatnasafn/Library of Water*. London: Artangel, 2007.

Horn, Roni. *Weather Reports You*. Göttingen, Germany: Artangel/Steidl, 2007.

Julien, Isaac. *Western Union: Small Boats*. 2007. Last modified 26 January 2018. https://www.isaacjulien.com/projects/western-union-small-boats/.

Junius Manuscript, The. Ed. George Philip Krapp. Anglo-Saxon Poetic Records 1. New York: Columbia University Press, 1931. Oxford, Bodleian Library, MS. Junius 11. Last modified 20 January 2019. https://iiif.bodleian.ox.ac.uk/iiif/viewer/d5e3a9fc-abaa-4649-ae48-be207ce8da15 – ?c=0&m=0&s=0&cv=6&r=0&xywh=-5830,-419,16482,8355.

Lee, S. D. Ed. *Ælfric's Homilies on 'Judith', 'Esther', and the 'Maccabees'* (1999). http://users.ox.ac.uk/~stuart/kings/.

Liuzza, Roy M. Ed. *Anglo-Saxon Prognostics: An Edition and Translation from Texts in London, British Library, MS Cotton Tiberius A.iii*. Cambridge: D. S. Brewer, 2011.

Maxims I. Eds. George Philip Krapp and Elliott Van Kirk Dobbie. In *The Exeter Book*, Anglo-Saxon Poetic Records 3. New York: Columbia University Press, 1936. 156–63.

Maxims II. Eds. Elliott Van Kirk Dobbie. In *The Anglo-Saxon Minor Poems*, Anglo-Saxon Poetic Records 6. New York: Columbia University Press, 1942. 55–7.

Meyer, Thomas. Trans. *Beowulf: A Translation*. Brooklyn, N.Y.: Punctum Books, 2012.

Monk, Geraldine. *They Who Saw the Deep*. Anderson, S.C.: Parlor Press, 2016.

Morris, Sharon. *Film in Space*, Camden Arts Centre. 2013.

Morris, Sharon. *Gospel Oak*. London: Enitharmon Press, 2013.

Morris, Sharon. *The Moon and a Smile*, Glynn Vivian Art Gallery, Swansea. 2017.

Morris, Sharon. *The Moon is Shining on My Mother*. London: Glynn Vivian Art Gallery with Enitharmon Editions, 2017.

Ob Rey, Philip. *"V" HS*. In *Humantropy*. 2015. Last modified 26 January 2019. http://www.humantropy.com/.

Paterson, Katie. *Langjökull, Snæfellsjökull, Solheimajökull*. 2007. Last modified 30 July 2018. http://katiepaterson.org/portfolio/langjokull-snaefellsjokull-solheimajokull/.

Paterson, Katie. *Future Library*. Last modified 25 June 2018. http://www.futurelibrary.no/.

Perry, Sondra. *Typhoon Coming On*. Serpentine Gallery, London. 2018. Last modified 26 January 2019. https://www.serpentinegalleries.org/exhibitions-events/sondra-perry-typhoon-coming-on.

Philip, M. NourbeSe. *Zong!* Middletown, Conn.: Wesleyan University Press, 2008.

Pope, John C. and R. D. Fulk. Eds. *Eight Old English Poems*. 3rd edn. New York: W.W. Norton, 2000.

Ruben, Abraham Anghik. Last modified 26 January 2019. http://www.abrahamruben.com/, http://www.abrahamruben.com/artwork/north-atlantic-saga/, http://www.abrahamruben.com/artwork/sedna-life-out-of-balance/.

Sharrocks, Amy. *The Museum of Water*. Last modified 7 January 2019. http://www.museumofwater.co.uk/.

Solnit, Rebecca. *The Faraway Nearby*. New York: Viking, 2013.

Stainer, Pauline. *Sleeping under the Juniper Tree*. Hexham, Northumberland: Bloodaxe Books, 2017.

Sweeney, Kate. *Antiphonal*. Last modified 7 January 2019. https//vimeo.com/katesweeney.

Waves and Bones. Part of 'Crossings: Newcastle Poetry Festival', 2018. Newcastle: Newcastle Centre for the Literary Arts, Newcastle University.

Weiner, Matthew. *Mad Men* (opening credits). Lionsgate, 2007. Last modified 30 July 2018. https://www.youtube.com/watch?v=WcRr-Fb5xQo.

Williamson, Craig. Ed. *The Old English Riddles of the Exeter Book*. Chapel Hill: University of North Carolina Press, 1977.

Williamson, Craig. Trans. *A Feast of Creatures: Anglo-Saxon Riddle-Songs*. Philadelphia: University of Pennsylvania Press, 1982.

Critical works

Addison, Kenneth. 'Changing Places: The Cistercian Settlement and Rapid Climate Change in Britain.' In *A Place to Believe In: Locating Medieval Landscapes*. Edited by Lees and Overing, 211–38.

Alfano, Christine. 'The Issue of Feminine Monstrosity: A Reevaluation of Grendel's Mother.' *Comitatus* 23.1 (1992): 1–16.

Allfrey, Francesca, Francesca Brooks, Joshua Davies, Rebecca Hardie, Carl Kears, Clare Lees, Kathryn Maude, James Paz, Hana Videen and Victoria Walker. 'New Ways to Know the Medieval: Creativity, Pedagogy and Public Engagement with *Colm Cille's Spiral*.' *Old English Newsletter* 46.3 (2015). Last modified 7 January 2019. http://www.oenewsletter.org/OEN/issue/46–3_allfrey.php.

Armstrong, Lily. '"Inscientibus pueralis, non senibus": Ælfric's Grammar out of Context in Oxford MS Barlow 35.' MSt dissertation, University of Oxford, 2018.

Baker, T. F. T., Diane K. Bolton and Patricia E. C. Croot. 'Hampstead: Settlement and Growth.' 'Hampstead: Hampstead Heath.' In *A History of the County of Middlesex: Volume 9, Hampstead, Paddington*. Edited by C. R. Elrington. London: Victoria County History, 1989, 8–15, 75–81. *British History Online*, http://www.british-history.ac.uk/vch/middx/vol9/pp8-15 and http://www.british-history.ac.uk/vch/middx/vol9/pp75-81.

Bammesberger, Alfred. 'The Place of English in Germanic and Indo-European.' In *The Cambridge History of the English Language. Volume I: The Beginnings to 1066*. Edited by Richard M. Hogg, 26–66. Cambridge: Cambridge University Press, 1992.

Bate, Jonathan. Ed. *The Public Value of the Humanities*. London: Bloomsbury Academic, 2011.

Bennett, Helen T., Clare A. Lees and Gillian R. Overing. 'Anglo-Saxon Studies, Gender and Power: Feminism in Old English Studies.' *Medieval Feminist Newsletter* 10 (1990): 15–24.

Berg, Maggie and Barbara K. Seeber. *The Slow Professor: Challenging the Culture of Speed in the Academy*. Toronto: University of Toronto Press, 2016.

Bergthaller, Hannes, Rob Emmett, Adeline Johns-Putra, Agnes Kneitz, Susanna Lidström, Shane McCorristine, Isabel Pérez Ramos, Dana Phillips, Kate Rigby and Libby Robin. 'Mapping Common Ground: Ecocriticism, Environmental History, and the Environmental Humanities.' *Environmental Humanities* 5.1 (2014): 261–76.

Bernstein, Charles. 'Caroline Bergvall's *Meddle English*.' Review. 13 July 2011. Last modified 15 June 2018. https://jacket2.org/commentary/caroline-bergvalls-meddle-english.

Bitterli, Dieter. *Say What I am Called: The Old English Riddles of the Exeter Book and the Anglo-Latin Riddle Tradition*. Toronto Anglo-Saxon Series 2. Toronto: University of Toronto Press, 2009.

Bosworth, J. and T. Northcote Toller. *An Anglo-Saxon Dictionary*. Oxford: Clarendon Press, 1898. T. Northcote Toller. *An Anglo-Saxon Dictionary, Based on the Manuscript Collections of the Late Joseph Bosworth: Supplement*. Oxford: Clarendon Press, 1921. http://bosworth.ff.cuni.cz. Last modified 30 January 2019.

Brooker, Will and Deborah Jermyn. Eds. *The Audience Studies Reader*. London: Routledge, 2003.

Brown, DeNeen L. 'Abraham Anghik Ruben, "the Intermediary": Sculptor Carves Inuit Legends of his Heritage.' *Washington Post*, 25 October 2012. Last modified 20 January 2018. http://www.washingtonpost.com/entertainment/museums/abraham-anghik-ruben-the-intermediarysculptor-carves-inuit-legends-of-his-heritage/2012/10/25/6fbbaf12-1d5d-11e2-b647-bb1668e64058_story.html.

Brown, Michelle. *The Lindisfarne Gospels: Society, Spirituality and the Scribe*. London: British Library, 2003.

Cameron, Angus, Ashley Crandell Amos, Antonette diPaolo Healey *et al. Dictionary of Old English: A to I* online. Dictionary of Old English Project, University of Toronto Centre for Medieval Studies, 2018. Last modified 30 January 2019. https://www.doe.utoronto.ca/pages/index.html.

Carlson, Signe M. 'The Monsters of *Beowulf*: Creations of Literary Scholars.' *Journal of American Folklore* 80.318 (1967): 357–64.

Carrigan, Mark and Filip Vostal. 'Not So Fast! A Critique of the "Slow Professor".' *University Affairs/ Affaires universitaires*, 22 April 2016. Last modified 25 June 2018. http://www.universityaffairs.ca/opinion/in-my-opinion/not-so-fast-a-critique-of-the-slow-professor/.

Cavell, Megan. *Weaving Words and Binding Bodies: The Poetics of Human Experience in Old English Literature*. Toronto: University of Toronto Press, 2016.

Cavill, Paul. *Maxims in Old English Poetry*. Cambridge: D. S. Brewer, 1999.

Cesario, Marilina. 'Weather Prognostics in Anglo-Saxon England.' *English Studies* 93.4 (2012): 391–426.

Clarke, Catherine A. M. 'Edges and Otherworlds: Imagining Tidal Spaces in Early Medieval Britain.' In *The Sea and Englishness in the Middle Ages*. Edited by Sobecki, 81–101.

Clarke, Catherine A. M. Ed. *Medieval Cityscapes Today*. Leeds: ARC Humanities Press, 2019.

Clegg Hyer, Maren and Della Hooke. 'Introduction.' In *Water and the Environment in the Anglo-Saxon World*. Edited by Clegg Hyer and Hooke, 1–14.

Clegg Hyer, Maren and Della Hooke. Eds. *Water and the Environment in the Anglo-Saxon World*. Liverpool: Liverpool University Press, 2017.

Cohen, Jeffrey Jerome. *Stone: An Ecology of the Inhuman*. Minneapolis: University of Minnesota Press, 2015.

Curzan, Anne. *Gender Shifts in the History of English*. Cambridge: Cambridge University Press, 2003.

D'Arcens, Louise. Ed. *The Cambridge Companion to Medievalism*. Cambridge: Cambridge University Press, 2016.

Davies, Joshua. *Visions and Ruins: Cultural Memory and the Untimely Middle Ages*. Manchester: Manchester University Press, 2018.

Dinshaw, Carolyn. *How Soon is Now? Medieval Texts, Amateur Readers, and the Queerness of Time*. Durham, N.C.: Duke University Press, 2012.

Donoghue, Daniel. *How the Anglo-Saxons Read Their Poems*. Philadelphia: University of Pennsylvania Press, 2018.

Ellard, Donna Beth. *Anglo-Saxon(ist) Pasts, postSaxon Futures*. Brooklyn, N.Y.: Punctum Books, 2019.

Elliott, Andrew B. R. *Medievalism, Politics and Mass Media: Appropriating the Middle Ages in the Twenty-First Century*. Woodbridge: D. S. Brewer, 2017.

Estes, Heide. *Anglo-Saxon Literary Landscapes: Ecotheory and the Environmental Imagination*. Amsterdam: Amsterdam University Press, 2017.

Foley, John Miles. *Traditional Oral Epic: The Odyssey, Beowulf and the Serbo-Croatian Return Song*. Berkeley: University of California Press, 1991.

Frederick, Jill. 'From Whale's Road to Water under the Earth: Water in Anglo-Saxon Poetry.' In *Water and the Environment in the Anglo-Saxon World*. Edited by Clegg Hyer and Hooke, 15–32.

Gill, Rosalind. 'Breaking the Silence: The Hidden Injuries of the Neoliberal University.' In *Secrecy and Silence in the Research Process: Feminist Reflections*. Edited by Rosalind Gill and Róisín Ryan-Flood. 228–44. Abingdon, Oxfordshire: Routledge, 2010.

Gross, Jonathan and Stephanie Pitts. 'Audiences for the Contemporary Arts: Exploring Varieties of Participation across Art Forms in Birmingham, UK.' *Participations: Journal of Audience & Reception Studies* 13.1 (May 2016): 4–23.

Hadfield, Andrew. 'The Summoning of Everyman.' In *The Oxford Handbook of Tudor Drama*. Edited by Thomas Betteridge and Greg Walker, 93–108. Oxford: Oxford University Press, 2012.

Heng, Geraldine. 'Color.' In *The Invention of Race in the European Middle Ages*, 181–256. Cambridge: Cambridge University Press, 2018.

Hilevaara, Katja and Emily Orley. Eds. *The Creative Critic: Writing as/about Practice*. London: Routledge, 2018.

Holden, John. *Cultural Value and the Crisis of Legitimacy: Why Culture Needs a Democratic Mandate*. London: Demos, 2006.

Holsinger, Bruce. 'Thorkel Farserk Goes for a Swim: Climate Change, the Medieval Optimum, and the Perils of Amateurism.' In *The Middle Ages in the Modern World: Twenty-First Century Per-*

spectives. Edited by Bettina Bildhauer and Chris Jones, 27–40. Oxford: Published for the British Academy by Oxford University Press, 2017.

Hooke, Della. 'Rivers, Wells and Springs in Anglo-Saxon England: Water in Sacred and Mystical Contexts.' In *Water and the Environment in the Anglo-Saxon World*. Edited by Clegg Hyer and Hooke, 107–35.

Karkov, Catherine E. *Text and Picture in Anglo-Saxon England: Narrative Strategies in the Junius 11 Manuscript*. Cambridge: University of Cambridge Press, 2001.

Karkov, Catherine E. Ed. *Slow Scholarship: Medieval Research & the Neoliberal University*. Essays and Studies 20. Cambridge: D. S. Brewer for the English Association, 2019.

Kears, Carl. 'Eric Mottram and Old English: Revival and Re-use in the 1970s.' *Review of English Studies* 69 (2018): 430–54.

Kreider, Kristen and James O'Leary (Kreider + O'Leary), *Falling*. Ventnor, Isle of Wight: Copy Press, 2015.

Leclercq, Jean. *Love of Learning and Desire for God: A Study of Monastic Culture*. 3rd edn. Translated by Catharine Misrahi. New York: Fordham University Press, 1982.

Lees, Clare A. 'Men and *Beowulf*.' In *Medieval Masculinities: Regarding Men in the Middle Ages*. Edited by Clare A. Lees. 129–48. Minneapolis: University of Minnesota Press, 1994.

Lees, Clare A. 'Basil Bunting, *Briggflatts*, Lindisfarne, and Anglo-Saxon Interlace.' In *Anglo-Saxon Culture and the Modern Imagination*. Edited by David Clark and Nicholas Perkins, 111–28. Cambridge: D. S. Brewer, 2010.

Lees, Clare A. Ed. *The Cambridge History of Early Medieval English Literature*. Cambridge: Cambridge University Press, 2013.

Lees, Clare A. 'In Three Poems: Medieval and Modern in Seamus Heaney, Maureen Duffy and Colette Bryce.' In *American/Medieval: Nature and Mind in Cultural Transfer*. Edited by Overing and Wiethaus, 177–201.

Lees, Clare A. 'A Word to the Wise: Men, Gender, and Medieval Masculinities.' In *Rivalrous Masculinities: New Directions in Medieval Gender Studies*. Edited by Rasmussen, 1–26.

Lees, Clare A. and Gillian R. Overing. *Double Agents: Women and Clerical Culture in Anglo-Saxon England*. Philadelphia: University of Pennsylvania Press, 2001; rev. edn Cardiff: University of Wales Press, 2009.

Lees, Clare A. and Gillian R. Overing. Eds. *A Place to Believe In: Locating Medieval Landscapes*. University Park: Pennsylvania State University Press, 2006.

Lees, Clare A. and Gillian R. Overing. 'Women and the Origins of English Literature.' In *The History of British Women's Writing, 700–1500*. Edited by Liz Herbert McAvoy and Diane Watt, 31–40. History of British Women's Writing 1. New York: Palgrave Macmillan, 2013.

Lees, Clare A. and Gillian R. Overing. 'Women and Water: Icelandic Tales and Anglo-Saxon Moorings.' *GeoHumanities* 4.1 (2018): 97–111.

Le Feuvre, Lisa. Ed. *Failure*. Documents of Contemporary Art. London: Whitechapel Gallery, 2010.

Levine, Caroline. *Forms: Whole, Rhythm, Hierarchy, Network*. Princeton, N.J.: Princeton University Press, 2015.

Leyerle, John. 'The Interlace Structure of *Beowulf*.' *University of Toronto Quarterly* 37.1 (1967): 1–17.

Lochrie, Karma, Clare A. Lees and Gillian R. Overing, 'Feminism Within and Without the Academy.' *Medieval Feminist Newsletter* 22 (1996): 27–31.

Lockett, Leslie. 'An Integrated Re-examination of the Dating of Oxford, Bodleian Library, Junius 11.' *Anglo-Saxon England* 31 (2002): 141–73.

Lockett, Leslie. 'The Junius Manuscript.' Last modified 20 January 2019. http://www.oxfordbibliographies.com/view/document/obo-9780195396584/obo-9780195396584-0145.xml.

Lykke, Nina. *Feminist Studies: A Guide to Intersectional Theory, Methodology and Writing*. London: Routledge, 2010.

MacCulloch, Diarmaid. *Silence: A Christian History*. New York: Viking, 2013.

Magennis, Hugh. 'Audience(s), Reception, Literacy.' In *A Companion to Anglo-Saxon Literature*. Edited by Phillip Pulsiano and Elaine Treharne, 84–101. Oxford: Blackwell Publishing, 2001.

Maitland, Sara. *A Book of Silence*. London: Granta, 2008.

Marcus, G. J. 'Hafvilla: A Note on Norse Navigation.' *Speculum* 30.4 (1955): 601–5.

Mills, Robert. *Derek Jarman's Medieval Modern*. Cambridge: D. S. Brewer, 2018.

Mittman, Asa Simon and Susan M. Kim. 'Locating the Devil *"Her"* in MS Junius 11.' *Gesta* 54.1 (2015): 3–25.

Moore, R. I. *The Formation of a Persecuting Society: Power and Deviance in Western Europe, 950–1250*. Oxford: Basil Blackwell, 1987.

Morris, Adalaide. 'Forensic Listening: NourbeSe Philip's "Zong!", Caroline Bergvall's "Drift", and the Contemporary Long Poem.' *Dibur Literary Journal* 4 (Spring 2017): 77–87.

Mountz, Alison, Anne Bonds, Becky Mansfield, Jenna Loyd, Jennifer Hyndman, Margaret Walton-Roberts, Ranu Basu, Risa Whitson, Roberta Hawkins, Trina Hamilton and Winifred Curran. 'For Slow Scholarship: A Feminist Politics of Resistance through Collective Action in the Neoliberal University.' *ACME: An International Journal for Critical Geographies* 14.4 (2015): 1235–59.

Mountz, Alison, Anne Bonds, Becky Mansfield, Jenna Loyd, Jennifer Hyndman, Margaret Walton-Roberts, Ranu Basu, Risa Whitson, Roberta Hawkins, Trina Hamilton and Winifred Curran. 'All for Slow Scholarship and Slow Scholarship for All.' *University Affairs/Affaires universitaires*, 9 May 2016. Last modified 25 June 2018. http://www.universityaffairs.ca/opinion/in-my-opinion/slow-scholarship-slow-scholarship/.

Murphy, Patrick J. *Unriddling the Exeter Riddles*. University Park: Pennsylvania State University Press, 2011.

Nicholson, Linda. Ed. *The Second Wave: A Reader in Feminist Theory*. London: Routledge, 1997.

Niles, John D. 'Ring Composition and the Structure of *Beowulf*.' *PMLA* 94.5 (1979): 924–35.

OED Online. *Oxford English Dictionary*. Oxford: Oxford University Press, 2019. Last modified 30 January 2019. http://www.oed.com/.

Oosthuizen, Susan. 'Culture and Identity in the Early Medieval Fenland Landscape.' *Landscape History* 37.1 (2016): 5–24.

Oosthuizen, Susan. *The Anglo-Saxon Fenland*. Oxford: Windgather Press, 2017.

Orchard, Andy. 'Enigma Variations: The Anglo-Saxon Riddle-Tradition.' In *Latin Learning and English Lore: Studies in Anglo-Saxon Literature for Michael Lapidge*, 2 vols. Edited by Katherine O'Brien O'Keeffe and Andy Orchard, vol. 1, 284–304. Toronto: University of Toronto Press, 2005.

Overing, Gillian R. *Language, Sign, and Gender in 'Beowulf'*. Carbondale: Southern Illinois University Press, 1990.

Overing, Gillian R. '*Beowulf* on Gender.' *New Medieval Literatures* 12 (2010): 1–22.

Overing, Gillian R. '*Beowulf*: A Poem in Our Time.' In *The Cambridge History of Early Medieval English Literature*. Edited by Clare A. Lees, 309–31. Cambridge: Cambridge University Press, 2013.

Overing, Gillian R. 'Men in Trouble: Warrior Angst in *Beowulf*.' In *Rivalrous Masculinities: New Directions in Medieval Gender Studies*. Edited by Rasmussen, 27–41.

Overing, Gillian R. and Cynthia Caywood. 'Writing across the Curriculum: A Model for a Workshop and a Call for Change.' In *Teaching Writing: Pedagogy, Gender, and Equity*. Edited by Cynthia Caywood and Gillian R. Overing, 185–200. Albany: State University of New York Press, 1987.

Overing, Gillian R. and Marijane Osborn. *Landscape of Desire: Partial Stories of the Medieval Scandinavian World*. Minneapolis: University of Minnesota Press, 1994.

Overing, Gillian R. and Ulrike Wiethaus. Eds. *American/Medieval: Nature and Mind in Cultural Transfer*. Göttingen, Germany: V&R unipress, 2016.

Overing, Gillian R. and Ulrike Wiethaus, 'Introduction: The Making of American/Medieval.' In *American/Medieval: Nature and Mind in Cultural Transfer*. Edited by Overing and Wiethaus, 9–23.

Overing, Gillian R. and Ulrike Wiethaus. Eds. *American/Medieval Goes North: Earth and Water in Transit*. Göttingen, Germany: V&R unipress, forthcoming 2019.

Paz, James. *Nonhuman Voices in Anglo-Saxon Literature and Material Culture*. Manchester: Manchester University Press, 2017.

Phelpstead, Carl. 'Beyond Ecocriticism: A Cosmocritical Reading of Ælfwine's Prayerbook.' *Review of English Studies* 69.281 (2018): 613–31.

Pinner, Rebecca. 'Thinking Wetly: Causeways and Communities in East Anglian Hagiography.' *Open Library of Humanities* 4.2 (2018): 2–49. DOI: http://doi.org/10.16995/olh.229.

Ramey, Peter. 'Crafting Strangeness: Wonder Terminology in the Exeter Book Riddles and the Anglo-Latin Enigmata.' *Review of English Studies* 69.289 (2017): 201–15.

Rasmussen, Ann Marie. Ed. *Rivalrous Masculinities: New Directions in Medieval Gender Studies*. Notre Dame, Ind.: University of Notre Dame Press, 2019.

Rendell, Jane. *Art and Architecture: A Place Between*. London: I. B. Tauris, 2006.

Reynolds, Rebecca. 'Food from the Water: Fishing.' In *Water and the Environment in the Anglo-Saxon World*. Edited by Clegg Hyer and Hooke, 136–51.

Rudolf, Winfried. 'The Spiritual Islescape of the Anglo-Saxons.' In *The Sea and Englishness in the Middle Ages*. Edited by Sobecki, 31–57.

Rylance, Rick. *Literature and the Public Good*. Oxford: Oxford University Press, 2016.

Saenger, Paul. *Space between Words: The Origins of Silent Reading*. Stanford, Calif.: Stanford University Press, 1997.

Salvador-Bello, Mercedes. *Isidorean Perceptions of Order: The Exeter Book Riddles and Medieval Latin Enigmata*. Morgantown: West Virginia University Press, 2015.

Snyder, R. Claire. 'What is Third-Wave Feminism? A New Directions Essay.' *Signs* 34.1 (2008): 175–96.

Sobecki, Sebastian I. Ed. *The Sea and Englishness in the Middle Ages: Maritime Narratives, Identity and Culture*. Cambridge: D. S. Brewer, 2011.

Sturtevant, Paul B. *The Middle Ages in Popular Imagination: Memory, Film and Medievalism*. London: I. B. Tauris, 2018.

Tripney, Natasha. Review of *Everyman*, National Theatre. *The Stage*, 30 April 2015. Last modified 20 January 2019. https://www.thestage.co.uk/reviews/2015/everyman-2/.

Verwoert, Jan. *Bas Jan Ader: In Search of the Miraculous*. London: Afterall Books, 2006.

Wallace, David. *Geoffrey Chaucer: A New Introduction*. Oxford: Oxford University Press, 2017.

Whalley, Bethany. 'Currents of History: Water and Waterways in Early Medieval Culture and the Contemporary Arts.' PhD thesis, King's College London, due to be submitted 2019.

Wickham-Crowley, Kelley M. 'Living on the *Ecg*: The Mutable Boundaries of Land and Water in Anglo-Saxon Contexts.' In *A Place to Believe In: Locating Medieval Landscapes*. Edited by Lees and Overing, 85–110.

Wickham-Crowley, Kelley M. 'Fens and Frontiers.' In *Water and the Environment in the Anglo-Saxon World*. Edited by Clegg Hyer and Hooke, 68–88.

Wieland, Gernot. 'Cædmon, the Clean Animal.' *American Benedictine Review* 35.2 (1984): 194–203.

Zuckerman, Esther. '*Mad Men* Stands at the Window.' *The Atlantic*, 21 June 2013. Last modified 30 July 2018. https://www.theatlantic.com/entertainment/archive/2013/06/mad-men-falling-man-finale/314016/.

Blogs

Bergvall, Caroline. 'Adventures in the Illuminated Sphere.' Whitechapel Gallery, London. Last modified 26 January 2019. https://www.whitechapelgallery.org/events/adventures-in-the-illuminated-sphere/.

Cavell, Megan. Ed. *The Riddle Ages: An Anglo-Saxon Riddle Blog*. Last modified 20 January 2019. https://theriddleages.wordpress.com/.

Contemplative Outreach blog. *Lectio Divina*. Last modified 30 July 2018. https://www.contemplativeoutreach.org/category/category/lectio-divina.

Ingraham, Chris. *Affect bibliography*. Last modified 20 January 2019. https://www.cdingraham.com/affect-bibliography.

Kokubun, Tetsuo. 'Horse Chestnut under Attack.' Last modified 20 June 2018. https://www.kew.org/blogs/kew-science/horse-chestnut-under-attack.

Lees, Clare A. and *Difference Exchange*. 'Colm Cille's Spiral.' Last modified 7 January 2019. http://www.colmcillespiral.net/ and https://www.kcl.ac.uk/cultural/-/Past-Projects/ColmCillesspiral.aspx.

Lees, Clare A. and Gillian R. Overing. 'Deep Water Tales.' *Midsummer Water Day*. King's College London. Last modified 7 January 2019. https://www.kcl.ac.uk/cultural/archive/culturalinstitute/showcase/past/pp/1314/talksevents/midsummer-water-day.aspx.

Index

Note: Page numbers in italics are figures; with 'n' are notes.

and self 76
waterways 86–9
see also Library of Water (Horn)
Water, Selected (Horn) 14, *76, 77, 78*
Waters, Ethel 53, 54
Waters, John 53–4
waves 17, 18, 19, 23, 85
Waves and Bones 3
wave theory 17
weather 21, 22, 61–2, 77–8, 79–80, 83–6, 88
Weather Reports You (Horn) 15, 62
Weiner, Matthew 41
wetlands 81–2
white American man 41, 42
Whitechapel Gallery, London 4
Wickham-Crowley, Kelley 80–1, 82
Wiethaus, Ulrike 3
Williamson, Craig 55, 60
women
  Anglo-Saxon 56
  anonymous 3
  in *Beowulf* 22

and early medieval clerical culture 23
and writing 17
'Women and Water: Icelandic Tales and Anglo-Saxon Moorings' (Lees and Overing) 20, 21, 54
wonder 56–8, 69
Wonderwater: Alice Offshore (Horn) 53–4, 75, 76, 95
'The Word' 2
The Word Exchange 56
'wordhoard' 96
'A Word to the Wise: Men, Gender, and Medieval Masculinities' (Lees) 21–2
World Trade Center, Twin Towers, New York 32, 41, 42

You Are the Weather (Horn) 14, 21, 62

Zong! (NourbeSe Philip) 95–6, 97
Zong (ship) 95, 97

Lightning Source UK Ltd.
Milton Keynes UK
UKHW020846200919

350086UK00002B/11/P